How To Fulfill Your Divine Destiny

Biblical Principles for Accomplishing God's Plan for Your Life

Kenneth W. Hagin

How To Fulfill Your Divine Destiny

Kenneth W. Hagin

Fourth Printing 2007

ISBN-13: 978-0-89276-738-0
ISBN-10: 0-89276-738-3

In the U.S. write:
Kenneth Hagin Ministries
P.O. Box 50126
Tulsa, OK 74150-0126
1-888-28-FAITH
www.rhema.org

In Canada write:
Kenneth Hagin Ministries
P.O. Box 335, Station D
Etobicoke (Toronto), Ontario
Canada, M9A 4X3
www.rhemacanada.org

Contents

Chapter 1
You Have a Divine Destiny

Every Christian has a divine destiny. The Word of God says, "'For I know the plans I have for you,' declares the Lord, 'plans to prosper you and not to harm you, plans to give you hope and a future'" (Jer. 29:11 *NIV*). You see, God has a plan and a purpose for your life.

If you want to fulfill your divine destiny, you must first realize and understand that you have a divine destiny. You will never fulfill what you don't know you have.

We are living in a time when our standard of living is going up, up, up. We enjoy mechanical conveniences and physical luxuries such as the world has never known. But no other generation that has ever lived on the face of the earth has had as many cares of life as our generation.

Never has any generation faced the perplexing problems we face today. Despite all of our efforts and technological advances, misery is being piled on top of misery. Famine and disease stalk many lands. Mankind, both as a whole and individually, stands in dire need.

However, the Word of God teaches we can change these things. The devil may have destined us for pain and sorrow, but we can change that destiny through faith in God. We, not God, hold the key to our own destiny and future. God has already done everything He's going to do for mankind. He has made a way of escape. Through the blood redemption of the Lord Jesus Christ, we can have faith to change our destiny while on this earth.

You and I have two choices: We can either fold our hands and succumb to complacency, or we can fulfill our divine destiny! Every day you are faced with these two choices. You may have been unconsciously choosing the first one. But now that you know God has a destiny for you, choose His way!

Faith To Change Your Destiny And Receive God's Best

The Bible is full of examples of people who had to face these same two choices. Circumstances had determined a particular destiny for them, but they used their faith to change their destiny. As we look at some of these examples, let's try to imagine the situation as each of them asked himself the question, "Where do I go from here?"

First, in Mark 10:46-52, we find the example of Bartimaeus who, when faced with these choices, decided to change his destiny. He chose to fulfill *God's* destiny for his life.

His destiny had been chosen for him through circumstances. He was blind. There were no welfare funds then, no vocational training for the visually challenged, no Braille system. So he sat at a gate beside the road to Jericho. Circumstances had relegated Bartimaeus to the lowest of the low — to the very pit and dregs of humanity — to begging.

Just for a moment, imagine Bartimaeus as he sits beside that road, holding up his little cup. People and animals pass by on the dirt road, and the dust settles on his clothes. As he smells the food some are eating, his stomach cries out for a morsel of bread. Still he sits there, waving his cup, hoping perchance a wealthy merchant or landowner will drop in a few coins so that he can make it another day.

One day Bartimaeus hears a commotion. There is a great stir in the air. A large crowd seems to be approaching Jericho. Bartimaeus grabs hold of the hem of someone's robe as it brushes against him. He shakes it and demands, "What's happening? What's happening?"

The person replies, "Oh, Bartimaeus, it's Jesus of Nazareth passing by. Don't get yourself excited. The crowd will be gone in a minute, and maybe you can even get a few coins from them."

Bartimaeus is faced with the question: "What do I do now?" In other words, "Where do I go from here?" He realizes that this is the Man who has been going about doing good and healing all who were sick and oppressed of the devil (Acts 10:38).

Bartimaeus realizes that this is his opportunity. What he does from this moment on does not rest in the hands of God — nor does it rest in the hands of religious leaders. What happens to him from this moment on rests solely with blind Bartimaeus himself!

The Word of God says, ". . . *faith cometh by hearing, and hearing by the word of God*" (Rom. 10:17). Faith that changes your destiny comes by hearing God's Word. John's Gospel states that the Word was made flesh and dwelt among us (John 1:14). That Word was Jesus Christ.

When Bartimaeus hears that the Word is passing by, faith leaps up in his heart. He asks himself, "Do I sit here and let the crowd go by and maybe accumulate a few coins? Or do I turn to the only real help mankind has ever known?"

It doesn't take Bartamaeus long to make up his mind and respond to that question. Jumping to his feet, he screams and hollers, ". . . *Jesus, thou Son of David, have mercy on me"* (Mark 10:47). And Jesus healed him!

Bartimaeus had the faith he needed to change his destiny in life. He made his choice, and his life was changed.

Now let's examine the account of the ten lepers found in Luke 17. Outcasts from society, these men lived outside the town. One day they saw Jesus entering their town, and they asked themselves, "Where do we go from here? We are bound with this loathsome disease. It is mutilating us and taking us to our graves."

They decided to go to Jesus. So when Jesus was passing by, they cried, ". . . *Jesus, Master, have mercy on us"* (v. 13). When Jesus saw them, He told them to go show themselves to the priests.

Jesus didn't say, "Be healed." He simply said, "Go show yourselves to the priests." There was no physical change in their condition; their healing had not manifested. And under Jewish law, the priests were the only ones who could pronounce lepers whole in the eyes of society.

As one man, the ten men turned in unison. They did not question for a moment whether or not they should go to the priests. Verse 14 says, *". . . And it came to pass, that, AS THEY WENT, they were cleansed* [or healed]." They were set free because they chose to use their faith to change their destiny.

And finally, in Mark chapter 5, we find two stories: 1) that of a man who came to Jesus asking prayer for his sick daughter; and 2) the story of the woman with the issue of blood.

The woman with the issue of blood had spent all that she had on doctors, seeking to get well. Yet she got no better, *". . . but rather grew worse"* (v. 26). Then she heard of Jesus and had to answer the question: *Where do I go from here?*

She said to herself, "I know what I'll do — I'll go touch His clothes. If I can touch His clothes, I'll be well!" But when she got to where Jesus was, she found a crowd surrounding Him. She had to decide if getting to Him was worth the struggle of pushing and shoving her way through the crowd.

How many times have we been in her position when the thing we wanted was out of our reach? Often we decide, "Oh, it's not worth it. I'll get it later."

But the woman with the issue of blood made her way through the crowd, touched Jesus' clothes, and was instantly healed.

We must not forget that while all of this was going on, Jairus was waiting for Jesus to accompany him to his home, where his daughter lay sick (vv. 22-24). Immediately after the great miracle of the healing of the woman with the issue of blood, a messenger came, tapped Jairus on the shoulder, and said, "Don't bother the Master any longer. Your daughter is dead. It's all over" (v. 35).

When these words were spoken, it was almost as if Jesus was reading Jairus' thoughts. Jesus said, "Don't be afraid. Only believe." At that moment, Jairus had a choice to make: Do I run home to my family, or do I just walk along leisurely with Jesus because He said not to fear?

Jairus made the right decision. He took Jesus at His Word and continued home with Jesus at a leisurely pace. And his daughter was raised from the dead (vv. 36-43).

In both of these examples we've looked at, someone had to ask the question that you must now ask yourself: "Where do I go from here?" The answer is up to you. And the answer you give will determine your direction.

Will you choose to stay in the situations and circumstances of life that you have perhaps always been in? Or will you choose to use your faith to move in the direction God has for you? God's direction leads to your divine destiny!

I'm not saying it will be easy or that things will happen overnight. Remember, this is a *fight* of faith (1 Tim. 6:12). And it's by faith and *patience* that we inherit the promises of God (Heb. 6:12)! Your flesh doesn't want to live by faith. But as your spirit gets stronger, you will have the victory every time!

How To Win the War
Between the Flesh and the Spirit

Your spirit gets stronger as you feed on God's Word. Don't do things just because *you* want to do them — that's being led by the flesh. Find out what God's Word has to say before you act.

Learn how to walk with God. Ask God, "Where do You want me to go from here?" Quit trying to put *your* plan into action. Put *His* plan into action and receive His best for your life.

If you know for certain that God told you to do something and you obey — even though it seems contrary to natural laws — there is no way you can fail, because God never fails.

It all comes back to the war between the natural (or carnal) and the spiritual. Anytime you ask yourself, "Where do I go from here?" — anytime you face a crisis — there will be a war between the natural and the spiritual. You'd better be smart enough to go the way your inner man wants it done, or you're doomed to fail.

You will never fulfill your divine destiny if you let your natural man and senses make your decisions and choose your direction. The Bible says, *"For to be carnally minded is death; but to be spiritually minded is life and peace"* (Rom. 8:6). Only if you choose the plan God has for you will you be able to fulfill your divine destiny.

There are two directions you can take. One is to press on with God. The second is to run back to something that you know is secure. But you'll never be what God wants you to be if you turn and run. On the other hand, if you press toward the mark and begin to confess who you are in Christ Jesus, things will turn out well for you.

Chapter 2
Leave the Past Behind

As you've seen in the previous chapter, you have a divine destiny. Once you realize this fact and make the decision to press on with God, you need to take care of some things *before* you begin the task of fulfilling your destiny.

The first thing you need to do is *to leave the past behind!* You will never be able to move forward in life until you let go of the past.

Paul says in Philippians 3:13,14: *"Brethren, I count not myself to have apprehended* [or obtained, excelled]: *but this one thing I do, forgetting those things which are behind, and reaching forth unto those things which are before, I press toward the mark for the prize of the high calling of God in Christ Jesus."*

I want you to see something here. The great Apostle Paul said, "I count not myself to have excelled." Then he went on to say that he forgot those things which were behind him. That's an interesting statement for this great man of God to make, because not only did Paul have to forget *success*, he also had to forget *failure!*

As he penned those words, I'm sure Paul's mind went back to the day he stood and held the coats of men and encouraged them as they were stoning Stephen (Acts 7:58-8:3).

Someone said, "I have trouble forgetting my past." Well, you weren't ever the catalyst who encouraged the stoning of one of God's chosen! You don't have to forget *that*, but Paul did.

Paul also had to forget his success in Athens with the great Greek philosophers. Paul proclaimed to them the great "philosophy" of the Gospel of the Lord Jesus Christ and many believed and were saved.

This event was a great success in Paul's life. Here was a man from Tarsus, an outpost of the Roman empire, standing on Mars Hill with the greatest philosophers in Greece — and he matches them word for word and argument for argument through the power of God (Acts 17:16-33). That was a great success. But Paul had to forget it.

Paul also had to forget that he started one of the largest churches in history — the Church at Ephesus. If you'll study the Bible, you'll find that the church had between 20,000 and 40,000 members! That's a pretty good-sized church!

Yet Paul said, "I count not myself to have accomplished anything, but this one thing I do — forgetting those things which are behind." Paul forgot success. He forgot failure. He forgot everything that happened to him in the past, because it was history. It couldn't do anything for him now even if he wanted it to.

'Reaching Forth' Involves Effort

Too many of us want to live in the past, feeding off some great meeting we attended. But we need to move on to the greater things God has for us in the future. That's going to take commitment.

Too many people do not realize what commitment means. Paul showed his commitment when he wrote, *"Brethren, I count not myself to have apprehended: but this one thing I do, forgetting those things which are behind, and REACHING FORTH. . ."* (Phil. 3:13). Reaching forth involves effort. That's spelled *w-o-r-k*.

Are you still interested in going on with God? It means work — reaching forth, straining, pushing, and striving. For what? For ". . . *the high calling of God in Christ Jesus"* (v. 14).

Paul said, *"I press toward the mark. . . ."* Well, when you're "pressing" to get something, you're putting out energy and effort.

You're going to find out very quickly whether you want to exert the effort it takes to be this kind of child of God or not, because the devil is going to fight you. You're going to have to decide between running back to your security or pressing toward the mark of the high calling of God in Christ Jesus. But when you make the decision to go with God, and you put God's Word down in your heart, there isn't any place for you to go but over the top!

So make the commitment today to forget both the failures and successes of the past and walk on in the higher things of God and His Word. Decide today to leave your past behind and to start pressing toward your destiny in Him!

Chapter 3
Get Acquainted With God

You have already seen that you have a divine destiny and that you must leave the past behind in order to press toward the future. Now you need to know something about your divine destiny.

It's important to know *who* God is before you study *what* God has planned for you. You get to know who God is the same way you would get to know anyone else — by getting acquainted with Him.

To get acquainted with someone, you've got to listen to him; you've got to hear what he says. Similarly, if you want to get acquainted with God, you've got to listen to Him and hear what He's saying. And you become acquainted with God through His Word.

Could I get acquainted with someone if the two of us just sat down, introduced ourselves, and stared at each other for three hours? How much could I know about that person doing that? How much could he know about me?

We're going to know each other's names and what we look like, but that's about all we're going to know about each other. But if we sat there for three hours conversing back and forth with one another, we'd know something about each other.

To get acquainted with God, we've got to read His Word, pray, then do some talking to Him — but not all the time. There are times when we've got to be quiet and let Him talk awhile.

A man once told me, "I don't ever hear God talk to me."

I said, "Well, do you ever talk to Him?"

He said, "I talk to Him continually — all the time."

I said, "That's the problem. You're never quiet long enough to listen!"

It's not enough to *talk* to God. We must also learn to *listen* to Him. We will never hear God talk to us until we are quiet long enough for His Spirit to speak to ours. We get acquainted with God by spending time in His Word and in prayer by waiting on Him. Only then will we become acquainted with God.

One of the first things we learn is that God is a Spirit (John 4:24). We hear this quoted from the Word. We tritely talk about it, and we mentally agree to it sometimes. But it's true. God, who is a

Spirit, is omnipresent: He is present everywhere all the time, existing everywhere simultaneously.

Knowing the Father

This omnipresent Spirit of God who is the same all over the world, can also commune with us on a one-to-one basis. We think about the awesomeness of God. We think about the power of God. We think about how big God is. Yes, God is all of that, but we also must realize that God is as personal with you and me as He is with every one of His children. That is a tremendous thought!

My children and grandchildren must be physically where I am if they're going to be in my presence. All of God's children can be in His Presence all the time no matter where they are. That's how big God is!

We need to get acquainted with God in these terms — in the intimacy of a Father-child relationship — not just in the awesome fact of His greatness.

You must also realize that you are a spirit; you have a soul; and you live in a body (1 Thess. 5:23). You understand and become acquainted with God through your spirit, not with your mind or body.

You cannot understand God with your intellect. That is what's wrong with the world today: People have tried to understand God and the things of God with their minds. That's why you see empty words with no power and no supernatural manifestations in so many churches. People are trying to understand God with the intellect.

In my office on the RHEMA Bible Training Center campus and in my study at home, I have textbook after textbook written by people with many degrees after their names. All of them talk about God and His family — but they're explaining it from a theological standpoint.

You could learn a little from these books, but you'll never really know God from them! You can study every theology book that's ever been written, but you'll still never know God from them. You'll know something *about* God, but you'll never *know* God.

You will never get acquainted with God until your spirit comes in contact with God's Spirit. Then you'll get acquainted with God!

The decision of how well you get acquainted with your Heavenly Father rests with you, because it's your spirit, not your mind, that has to be in full contact with God. You don't become acquainted with God by what you hear, what you see, what you read, or by your emotions. You get to know God by your spirit coming into contact with God's Spirit.

That's where the real knowledge of God takes place — in your spirit or heart, not just in your mind or intellect.

And there aren't enough demons in hell, there is no sickness, and no economic condition that can keep the children of God from fulfilling their divine destiny when they know who their Heavenly Father is. When God's children are acquainted with Him, there is no way they can be defeated. They are successes and conquerors in Christ Jesus!

Understanding Our Inheritance

So many Christians talk about being "King's kids." They know Jesus, their elder Brother. But they've never really gotten acquainted with God Himself, the Father. They don't know who He is, who He really is to us, and why we were created.

Why did God create man? He created man to have someone to fellowship with — someone to give His inheritance to. That's what the Bible teaches. God said in Genesis 1:26, ". . . *Let us make man in our image. . . .*" He made man to fellowship with Him.

It's exciting to know that we have a divine destiny, but before we run off to discover it, we should take the time to get to know the One who gave us the destiny in the first place. Sometimes we get excited about the inheritance we have in God, but we don't know the Creator who gave it to us in the first place. We must understand what that inheritance is: God has given us salvation.

> **JOHN 3:16**
> **16 For God so loved the world, that he gave his only begotten Son, that whosoever believeth in him should not perish, but have everlasting life.**

Knowing that God is love is getting acquainted with God (1 John 4:8). He loved so much, that He gave.

When you get acquainted with God, you will no longer be concerned about the "big I" — what "I" can get. No, when you start acting like the Father, because you know Him, you will be concerned about others instead of just about yourself. You will realize that everything you need and want has already been taken care of.

What Did 'Daddy' Say?

Let's look at that from a natural standpoint. I am the son of a fantastic man of God. As I grew up, I gave myself to help take care of the family, the cars, the yard, and the house. I didn't do it because

I was told, "Son, go mow the yard," or "Son, do this, that, and the other." No, when I saw that the garage needed to be cleaned out, I cleaned out the garage. When I saw that the yard needed to be mowed, I mowed the yard. When I saw that the house needed to be painted, I got some paint and painted the house. When I saw that the car needed to be washed, I washed the car. (I didn't wash it only when I wanted to go on a date — I tried to take care of it all the time!)

I noticed that when I began to do this, I didn't have to keep asking, "Dad, can I do this? Can I have that? I need this. I need that." I noticed that those things started being taken care of.

The Word of God says, *"If ye then, being evil* [or natural], *know how to give good gifts unto your children, how much more shall your Father which is in heaven give good things to them that ask him?"* (Matt. 7:11).

When you get acquainted with God, you realize that God has given you the good gifts of salvation, prosperity, and healing. (We will discuss these gifts in more detail in the next chapter.)

Scholars can write all the theological books they want against these gifts, but we've got to get to the point where we believe, like a little child does, that if "Daddy" — our Father God — said it, that's it. Nobody is ever going to be able to tell us any different.

I remember as I was growing up, when my father told me something, I believed him implicitly. And I know that after I've told my son, Craig, something, a thousand people could tell him it isn't so, but he would stand there and say, "I don't care what you say. My daddy said it is so."

Well, I'm going to stand up and say the same thing: "Believe what you want; write what you want; do what you want; but my Heavenly Father said that I was saved, delivered, healed, and set free! I'm going to go by what my Father says!"

God said in His Word that He will give us all the desires of our heart. When we get acquainted with God, we will know that we can have all of our needs and desires met: *"But my God shall supply all your need according to his riches in glory by Christ Jesus"* (Phil. 4:19).

You see, you just need to believe what God says about you. Then no matter what anyone else says or what circumstances may be saying to you, you can believe that what God has said is true, and you can continue to press toward your divine destiny. But in order to *believe* what God says about you in His Word, you must first *know* what His Word says!

So get acquainted with God. Know Him. Know Him through the Word. Converse with Him. Then once you do, you've got to agree with Him. Jesus said in Matthew 18:19, ". . . *if two of you shall agree on earth as touching any thing that they shall ask, it shall be done for them of my Father which is in heaven.*" When you and God come into agreement on His Word, Heaven and earth will move!

It's simple. It's not complex. Just get acquainted with God.

You must first get acquainted with Him through salvation. If you are not saved — if you have never accepted Jesus Christ as your Savior — you can do so today! And you don't have to do anything or give up anything to be saved. Just come to Him as you are.

Others may be acquainted with God through salvation, but not through the infilling of the Holy Spirit. They need to get acquainted with God in this way. He will become more real to them and will minister to them as they do.

As we read in the Book of Job, we find that we will not be disappointed when we acquaint ourselves with God.

JOB 22:21 (*Amplified*)
21 Acquaint now yourself with Him [agree with God and show yourself to be conformed to His will] and be at peace; by that [you shall prosper and great] good shall come to you.

The Word says, *"Heaven and earth shall pass away, but my words shall not pass away"* (Matt. 24:35). That's God's Word. So get acquainted with God and His Word. By conforming yourself to His will and according to His Word, you shall prosper and great good will come to you! And in God's Word, you *can* discover and fulfill your divine destiny!

Chapter 4
Discover Your Divine Destiny

Now that we've seen that every Christian has a divine destiny, let's take a more in-depth look into God's Word and see what it says concerning our destiny. One way we could define "destiny" is *God's will for our lives.*

Many people want to know what God's will is. Well, God's will is His Word!

As you get into the Word of God, you will learn that much of it is written in the past tense. In other words, it already has been accomplished. For example, First Peter 2:24 says, *"Who his own self bare our sins in his own body on the tree, that we, being dead to sins, should live unto righteousness: by whose stripes ye WERE HEALED."* (What we are in Christ, *who we are* in Christ, and *what we have* because of Him is for right *now*, not in the future, because *He has already done the work!*)

You can put our benefits in Christ in the future tense if you want to, but I'm going to start enjoying them *now* — as a reality *today!*

People sing about the "Sweet By-and-By" and talk about the "pie in the sky." Well, I'm excited about Heaven, too, but what I'm really interested in are the things that can do me some good *now* — right here — in the situations I'm facing *today*!

Yes, Heaven is great, and the promise of Heaven is wonderful; but it's not going to do you much good in the life you're living right now. It's not going to do you much good in the economic or political situations that confront you in today's world.

People can talk calamity all they want to. They can talk economic unrest all they want to. They can fill the radio, television, and newspapers full of that kind of talk. But I'm not going to walk around "cowed down" with a disappointed look on my face.

I don't care what the political scene says. I don't care what the economic scene says. *The Word of God* says I am more than a conqueror in Christ Jesus! It's past tense. Jesus said, *". . . be of good cheer; I have overcome the world"* (John 16:33). It already has happened. I can walk as a victor and a conqueror.

My God said that all of my needs are supplied according to His riches in glory (Phil. 4:19). Even if I don't know *how* God will do it, I know He will send me a supply to meet all of my needs!

Answer: HIPS, PHIS, SHIP

PAGE-A-DAY®CALENDAR | WWW.PAGEADAY.COM | WORKMAN PUBLISHING

FOUR-LETTER SHUFFLE

The word below has three useful anagrams. Can you find all of them?

P₃ I₁ S₁ H₄

8

Past, Present, or Future?

He already has said it. He's already done it. It's in the past tense. I'm not going to put it over in the future and begin to doubt what God has done for me. I'm going to receive it as already done. I'm going to live for God and have a great time doing it!

Galatians 3:13 says, *"Christ HATH redeemed us from the curse of the law. . . ."* Is "hath" past tense or future tense? It's past tense, isn't it?

The Word of God puts our redemption from the curse in the *past* tense. We can receive our deliverance because it's in the past tense. It already has been taken care of. It's not up to God now; it's up to you. You have the responsibility to receive from God what He says already belongs to you. It's up to you to receive what God has already done and to take it by faith *out of the past tense* and put it *into the present tense* so it can work for you.

Take hold of the destiny God has for you by receiving all that He's already provided for you through His Son, Jesus. *What you do with the past tense of God's Word will determine the future of your life!*

Look at Isaiah 53:4: *"Surely he HATH BORNE our griefs, and CARRIED our sorrows. . . ."* Are those verbs in the past tense? Yes.

Look at Matthew 8:17, *". . . Himself TOOK our infirmities, and bare our sicknesses."* Is the word "took" past, present, or future tense? "Took" and "bare" are past tense. Because He took our infirmities in the *past*, we can claim the promise *now* and take it into the present — because it is ours.

For example, look at the scripture, *". . . by whose stripes ye WERE healed"* (1 Peter 2:24). "Were" is past tense. Therefore, if we "were" healed, we *are* healed. Hallelujah!

You see, you don't have to wait for someone to lay hands on you to be healed. You don't have to wait for someone to pray for you. When you find out that God's Word has already made healing your divine destiny, then you can jump out of bed! You can begin to shout and rejoice — because you *were* and *are* healed!

Most people are sitting around waiting for the manifestation in this *natural* realm before they ever believe what God has already done in the spirit realm. Most people are sitting around waiting for their lives to change, but they're not doing anything to change them! Well, your destiny will not fulfill itself!

If the Word of God is going to do you any good, you've got to bring it into the present tense of your life *by faith*. Faith is now! Faith says, "It's mine; I have it now!" Once you get it into the present tense, then it will change your future.

When the Word of God talks about past-tense facts, if we would add a little practical knowledge and bring it into the present tense, our lives would be changed. Destinies would be changed. But it's up to us to make it happen.

Mark 11:24 says, ". . . *WHEN ye pray, BELIEVE that ye RECEIVE them* [what things soever you desire], *and ye shall have them.*" Notice it doesn't say, "Believe that you are *going* to receive them" (future tense). No, it says you *shall receive* them (present tense).

We must realize that God's past-tense Word can only become present tense in our lives when we act upon it. Even though He's already done it, *God can't do anything about it in our lives until we do.*

I realize that some people don't like hearing that, but if God has already done something about it, then His responsibility has ended and ours has begun.

Do you realize that God has entered into a contract with us? He has already taken care of all the stipulations. Even though He wants us to have what belongs to us, He cannot force it on us. *We must take responsibility and act on our knowledge of God's Word.*

You Can Have It Now!

You can talk about how much you want to be healed or filled with the Holy Spirit. You can say, "Well, I believe I'm going to be healed *sometime*," or "I believe I'm going to be filled *sometime*." But until you actually *act* on God's Word, you never will receive a thing.

Jesus Christ Himself demonstrated this when He raised Lazarus from the dead. One of Jesus' best friend was lying dead in a cave. Jesus stood outside that tomb and, while Lazarus was still dead, said, ". . . *Father, I thank thee that thou HAST heard me*" (John 11:41).

That's past tense. Jesus *didn't* say, "I thank Thee that Thou art *going* to hear Me." He said, "*Thou hast heard Me.*"

Yet there had been no manifestation. Lazarus was still dead, but Jesus was thanking His Heavenly Father that His prayer *had been heard*. Lazarus didn't stay dead very long, did he?

The sick who are believing for healing need to say, "Father, I thank Thee that Thou *hast* heard me," before healing ever materializes. As Mark 11:24 says, ". . . *WHEN* ye pray, *BELIEVE* that ye receive . . . *and ye shall have. . . .*"

Get hold of the past tense of God's Word. When you do, you will discover your divine destiny. Your divine destiny is *everything that God wants you to be and to have right now in the present and in the future.* And these things are determined by all that He has *already done in the past.* You can discover your divine destiny by finding out who the Word of God says you are, what the Word says you can have, and what the Word says you can do.

Then believe that these things are so *right now* before you see any of it with your natural eyes. With your natural eyes you see only temporal, material things. But with the eyes of your spirit, you can begin to behold supernatural, satisfying, lasting realities of God's spiritual, eternal Kingdom as you begin to fulfill your divine destiny.

I have a son, Craig, and a daughter, Denise. When they were younger, Craig got a pair of jogger skates — skates on tennis shoes — for Christmas.

Denise said, "Daddy, if I learn to skate, will you buy me some jogger skates?"

I said, "I sure will."

She took her brother's old skates that were about three sizes too big, went outside on the sidewalk, and learned to skate.

That put the responsibility back on Daddy. And I'm going to tell you something, I was not going to disappoint that girl! I told her that if she would learn to skate, I would buy her skates. And I wasn't going to lie to her. So I took time out of my schedule, went to the store, and bought her those skates.

God has already said that if you would do certain things, you would get certain results. He's already done His part. The Promiser has already promised something. *Now it's up to us to believe Him and make it happen.*

Chapter 5
Attend to God's Word

In the last chapter, we talked about what to do with the past tense of God's Word. Well, in order to make something happen and realize the fulfillment of God's Word, you have to know what God's Word says.

The only way you will learn what His Word says is by reading it. The amount of attention you give to the Bible will determine whether or not you fulfill your divine destiny. So you must *meditate in the Word.*

I'm not talking about grabbing your Bible for five minutes and turning to the Proverbs and Psalms for a scripture nugget. That's what some people call reading and studying the Word. They think five minutes' reading and a quick prayer is all they need to do each day.

Meditate in the Word

Joshua said, *"This book of the law shall not depart out of thy mouth; but thou shalt MEDI-TATE therein day and night, that thou mayest observe to do according to all that is written therein: for then thou shalt make thy way prosperous, and then thou shalt have good success"* (Joshua 1:8).

Another translation reads, ". . . and then shalt thou be able to deal wisely with the affairs of life."

How can you be a success if you can't deal wisely with the affairs of life? The thing most lacking among church people, in general, is wisdom.

Wisdom is necessary in all areas of life, even in the business world. If wisdom abounds, you will operate your business wisely. If you don't have any wisdom, you'll operate your business unwisely, and it will probably fail.

For example, if you are a store owner and your first store is barely making it, do you go out and open three more? No, that would be unwise, wouldn't it? You would need extra capital to carry the new stores until they get going.

Some people try to be too "spiritual" in their business affairs. For example, they launch out without using intelligence, saying, "Well, God will take care of me." No, God gave us a mind to use — to combine the natural with the supernatural or spiritual.

Success is not measured by anyone else. Success is not measured by your peers or by any other church or church member.

God once told me, "You're successful if you're doing what I told you to do, whether you've got three or three thousand people in your church. If you're doing what I told you to do, then you're successful."

If you're doing what God told you to do, whether it's working with children, teaching a Sunday school class, ushering, or otherwise helping in the church, then you are successful — no matter what friends, relatives, or neighbors may say.

Some may ask you, "If you're called to the ministry, why don't you go out there?" But maybe you're not supposed to go out into the fivefold ministry yet; maybe you're supposed to stay in the church and help for a while.

God does not compare you with anyone else. I know that from studying the Word of God and from being a parent. Do you measure the success of one child by what another child is doing? Or do you judge them on their own merits? Did you know God does the same? He judges our success on our own merits.

Another way to successfully fulfill your divine destiny is found in Psalm 1:1, *"Blessed is the man that walketh not in the counsel of the ungodly. . . ."*

News commentators and financial analysts make their predictions through the media, telling you, "Now's the time to do this; now's the time to do something else. Buy, sell, borrow, lend. . . ."

Often we can follow their lead — unless God is speaking to us to do otherwise. If we disregard His leading at such times, we cannot be blessed, because we're taking the counsel of the ungodly. We've got to use godly wisdom in these circumstances.

I remember one time God spoke to us to do a certain thing in this ministry. We had a meeting with our business advisers, who are all Spirit-filled Christian businessmen.

My dad, Rev. Kenneth E. Hagin, and I said to them, "We know what the economy says. We know what all of the business indicators say concerning the next few months. But God is saying something else to us about moving into a large project."

One of the men spoke up and said, "Brother Hagin, the Word of God that you teach says to move with God and not pay any attention to the counsel of the ungodly when God is speaking. I'm a businessman, and I've put these principles into practice. I pray about business decisions, and if God says do it — even if the business indicators say not to — I'll go ahead and do it. That's why I am where I am today."

He continued, "If I can't get an answer about something when I pray, I look to the economic indicators. If the indicators say, 'Don't do it,' I don't do it."

That's using natural and spiritual wisdom together. I'm not talking about double-mindedness; I'm talking about how to learn to use the natural and the supernatural together to become an explosive force for God.

Too many people throw intellect out the window when they start walking by faith, trying to be a success for God.

PSALM 1:1-3
1 Blessed is the man that walketh not in the counsel of the ungodly, nor standeth in the way of sinners, nor sitteth in the seat of the scornful.
2 But his delight is in the law of the Lord; and in his law doth he meditate day and night.
3 And he shall be like a tree planted by the rivers of water, that bringeth forth his fruit in his season; his leaf also shall not wither; and whatsoever he doeth shall prosper.

This passage sounds like Joshua 1:8, doesn't it? It means that when wintertime comes, the man or woman who obeys this passage is not going to dry up when the sap goes and the leaves fall. That gives you a picture of what happens when hard times come to the tree.

In winter, when the sap is not running and goes back down into the roots of the tree, that tree — unless it's an evergreen — looks like it's dead. But the life is in the foundation or roots of the tree. There is a root system beneath the tree that's deep enough and strong enough to support its height. All the life is there. That tree is just as much alive during winter as it is during any other time of the year; it just doesn't look like it.

It says here in Psalm 1 that the man who walks in the way of the Lord and meditates in the Word will bring forth fruit in his season, and his leaf shall not wither or fade away. And whatsoever he does will prosper.

Practice the Word

Another important point to consider is that God's Word does not change. It's the same today as it was yesterday. It will be the same tomorrow as it is today. It never changes.

Because God's Word never changes, we must not only meditate in it, we must *practice it!* Meditating in God's Word is easy. Putting what we've learned into practice is a different story!

For example, if you don't want your conscience pricked, don't study James. It seems that every time I start reading the Book of James, I come away with my ears red and burning, because he has turned me every way but loose! I have to take an inventory and straighten up. I tell you, James is written for strong Christians! (That's why many people never get involved with reading James.)

You can look in most people's Bibles and find Romans and Corinthians all marked up, along with some passages in First and Second Peter and First, Second, and Third John, and all the Gospels. But if you'll look over in James and Jude, you won't find many markings, because most people don't get in there very often!

James says to be a doer of the Word. It says, "... *shew me thy faith without thy works, and I will shew thee my faith by my works*" (James 2:18).

If you're going to have faith, it's got to have some legs, some arms, some muscle. You've got to *do* something; you can't just sit around.

A lot of people sit around, hollering that they want this, that, and the other, but they're not *doing* anything. They say, "I'm believing God for finances," but when the offering plate comes around, they turn up their nose and don't give.

Another fellow who is believing God, says, "Oh, thank God for meeting my financial needs. Lord, I've only got fifty cents, but here it is." That fellow will start climbing and climbing, and soon he'll be on top. The man who's not giving will still be hollering, "Oh, I'm confessing that God's going to meet my needs." By this time he has even less than he had before. Why? Because he's not *doing* anything that God can bless.

Put the Word First

I often see people sitting around doing nothing, "sleeping" on the church pew, getting spiritually fat and lazy until they become stagnant. Every so often, they holler, "Amen." This is a good description of a man who's not practicing the Word.

James says, *"For if any be a hearer of the word, and not a doer, he is like unto a man beholding his natural face in a glass: For he beholdeth himself, and goeth his way, and straightway forgetteth what manner of man he was"* (James 1:23,24).

Some people are trying to get by on the Word they learned twenty years ago. I'm not interested in the "good old days" or even the future. I'm interested in the here and *now*. I need help for my hurts *now*. I need something *now* — not "pie in the sky" in the future. And I'm not interested in what happened to someone twenty years ago. I want to know what can happen to me *now*.

Jesus Christ said that if we'd get into the Word, we could have success in our lives *now*.

In this chapter we have looked at different steps to take to fulfill our divine destiny and become a success in life. In review, you must first *meditate in the Word*; and second, you must *practice the Word*.

A third step to fulfilling your divine destiny and being a success in life is *to put the Word first in your life*. Become Word-conscious. Let the Word reign supreme in your life. No matter what comes, think about the Word first.

We all face tests and trials. When these crises and emergencies come in the natural — and they will come, whether your name is Hagin, Smith, or Jingleheimer — the person who is well-versed in the Word will start recalling pertinent scriptures. They'll start ringing in his head like a drum. If he faces illness, for example, he'll immediately hear scriptures such as First Peter 2:24: *"Who his own self bare our sins in his own body on the tree, that we, being dead to sins, should live unto righteousness: by whose stripes ye were healed."*

If he faces an ugly situation, in which he is tempted to be unloving or unforgiving, scriptures on love will start to roll on the inside of him.

I believe we can be so saturated with God's Word that the first thing that comes to mind in any emergency is not, "What are we going to do now?" but, "What does the Word say?" Very few people have reached that place. But it's crucial that we continually strive toward it; otherwise, we will never fulfill our divine destiny.

We must know what God has already done for us and has given to us. We must find out what our destiny is according to the Word of God. The only way to do this is to attend — *meditate* — on the Word.

We cannot sit around and wait for our destiny to fulfill itself. We must discover our destiny and then make it a reality!

Well, we know that God wants everyone to be saved. We read in God's Word that He wants all men to be saved and to come unto the knowledge of the truth (1 Tim. 2:4). And John 3:17 says, *"For God sent not his Son into the world to condemn the world; but that the world through him might be saved."* So we know from the Word that salvation is part of everyone's divine destiny.

Just as salvation has already been provided for us, so has health and prosperity. We know that salvation, health, and prosperity are part of our destiny because the Bible says that God has set us free from the law of sin and death (Rom. 8:2). That means that we have been set free from everything that is caused by sin — which includes sickness, disease, and poverty!

However, we will only know this is our destiny as we read the Word of God. And then the only way it will do *you* any good is when you *accept* and act on what God has already made available.

The only reason you weren't saved earlier than you were wasn't God's fault. God had already purchased salvation. The responsibility was yours to accept what already belonged to you.

God has already purchased healing. It's your responsibility to accept it.

God has already supplied all of your needs. It's your responsibility to act like it's so.

God has already done everything He's going to do about the devil. It's your responsibility to walk in the light and liberty of God's Word.

Friend, the devil has to run when he sees a child of God who knows who he is in Christ, because he knows he has already been defeated.

But the devil is not going to run from a child of God who is "cowed down," beaten down, and who is not taking his rightful place in the Word of God and living in what belongs to him.

The devil is going to keep heaping problems on him until that individual — not God — stands up and says, "Look, Mr. Devil, you have already been defeated. Now I'm going to walk in my rights and privileges as a born-again child of God."

The Constitution of the United States has already provided certain liberties and freedoms for us. If you don't live in those liberties, someone could lord it over you. If you don't claim those liberties, someone could try to tell you, "You can't have church. You have no right to worship as you choose."

People tried to tell my father-in-law that he couldn't build a church in a certain place. My father-in-law said, "What do you mean, I can't build a church here? It's my constitutional right to have a church. The people in this community want this church. It's their constitutional right to have this church."

A few people got a petition signed and took it to the city council. When it got there, the city planning commissioner said, "You people are in error. The Constitution of our land provides that these people can have a place to worship in." And that's all there was to it.

But you see, if my father-in-law had folded under their attack and said, "Well, I guess we can't have a church here," they never would have had it.

What did he do? He appropriated that which already had been provided.

This same kind of scenario can happen with the devil. As long as you say, "Well, I guess that's the way it is. I thought I could be healed, but I guess I can't," he'll just keep coming at you.

But when you turn around, straighten up, and say, "I am a new creature in Christ Jesus. It is written, 'I have authority over you,'" then you will begin to walk in liberty, and the devil will begin to run like a scared pup. Why? Because *you learned to use the principle of the past tense of God's Word.*

Take what God already has offered you and run with it like a dog would with a bone. Live in the liberty and happiness that belong to you by walking in the light of God's Word!

Chapter 6
Be Led by the Spirit of God

We've talked about steps to take to become a success in life. Another important step toward being a success in life is to *instantly obey the voice of God*.

The education and development of our human spirit comes by instantly obeying the voice of the Spirit. Proverbs 20:27 says, *"The spirit of man is the candle of the Lord...."* Romans 8:14 says, *"For as many as are led by the Spirit of God, they are the sons of God."*

God leads us by our *spirit*, not our *mind*. God informs our spirit, and our spirit informs our mind.

If you're going to be successful in life and fulfill your divine destiny, you've got to learn how to be led by the voice of God. However, not everyone who says, "God told me to do this" really heard from God. God is getting blamed for a lot of things He never did.

Unfortunately, there are many in charismatic circles saying, "God told me to do such-and-such," and God really hasn't told them to do it. They're doing it because that's what they want to do, so they say God told them to do it.

I've never done anything God told me to do that's ever failed. But I've seen a lot of other people get into a mess over what they *said* God told them to do. Actually, it was only what *they* wanted to do, and they said God told them to do it.

Others actually say, "God told me to do such-and-such" because they think it will carry more weight and importance, and will make people submit to their leadership.

You'd better be careful saying God told you to do something unless you know beyond a shadow of a doubt that God said to do it. You can get yourself into trouble saying that. You'd better be sure that it is God telling you to do something.

Some people say, "The devil made me do it." No, the devil didn't make you do it; you did it because you *willed* to do it. You've got a will of your own. You can control your destiny by the choices you make.

Obey Immediately the Voice of God's Spirit

There's a fine line to follow here. Be careful when you say that God told you to do something. But on the other hand, when God does speak, learn to follow that inward voice immediately — not tomorrow or next week — *immediately*. When God speaks to you, you'd better act immediately, even if you've got something else planned.

Do you want to be wise and have good success in life? Do you want to fulfill your divine destiny? Then find out what the Word of God has to say.

Practice it.

Do it.

Live by it.

Then get involved immediately with it as the Lord speaks.

Chapter 7
Learn To Forgive

We have seen the importance of attending to God's Word and being led by the Spirit of God. We know that in God's Word we find many provisions already made for us. I have shared with you some of what God has already done — the *past tense* of God's Word.

If God has already provided salvation, healing, and prosperity for anyone who will receive them, then what must *you* do to receive these provisions and make your destiny a *reality*? In these next few chapters I want to talk to you about what you need to do to receive all that God has for you.

MARK 11:22-24
22 And Jesus answering saith unto them, Have faith in God.
23 For verily I say unto you, That whosoever shall say unto this mountain, Be thou removed, and be thou cast into the sea; and shall not doubt in his heart, but shall believe that those things which he saith shall come to pass; he shall have whatsoever he saith.
24 Therefore I say unto you, What things soever ye desire, when ye pray, believe that ye receive them, and ye shall have them.

People get excited about these three verses. These verses tell us what we can get from God, what God can do for us, and how we can use our faith to receive.

Nearly everyone stops reading with Mark 11:24, but this discourse which the Master started in verse 22 doesn't end with verse 24!

In the following verses, Jesus makes two more statements that are vitally important for faith. The first is in verse 25:

MARK 11:25
25 And WHEN YE STAND PRAYING, FORGIVE, if ye have ought against any; that your Father also which is in heaven may forgive you your trespasses.

Jesus ties this thought to verse 24 with a conjunction. If this had been edited correctly in King James' time, there would not be a period after "them" in verse 24; there would be a comma and then the word "and" joining the two thoughts. These two verses were meant to go together.

Most people stop reading at the end of verse 24 and get all excited about receiving the things they desire. But there's more to it than that. Verse 25 goes on to talk about things that can hinder our faith and prayers.

Forgive and Forget

Notice in verse 25 that the Father calls holding grudges against our fellow man "trespasses." This is serious. When you study the various translations, you will see you need to forgive so that your Father can forgive your sins. Really, it is a sin to hold grudges against people.

People say, "Well, I can *forgive*, but I'll never *forget* what was done to me." That's not forgiving. I once heard a man say, "I know I have to forgive in order for God to meet my needs. I tell you what, I'm going to forgive the person who wronged me, but I'm never going to forget what he did to me."

You have to let it drop and forget it, no matter what someone's done to you. *The Amplified Bible* says, "And whenever you stand praying, if you have anything against anyone, forgive him and let it drop...."

"Yeah, but you don't know what they did to me," someone will protest.

Has anyone killed you yet? Has he hung you on a cross yet? When they nailed Jesus to the cross of Calvary, He said, "Father, forgive them, because they don't understand what they are doing" (Luke 23:24).

When someone says something about you that you don't like, you might say, "I'm not going to let them get away with that! They're not going to make *me* look like a fool and get away with it!" Then soon afterwards you might say, "Oh, thank God, I'm confessing that God will meet all of my needs."

How in the world can God meet your needs according to His Word when you're not living in line with *His Word?* Look at what He says in verse 26.

> **MARK 11:26**
> **26 But if ye do not forgive, neither will your Father which is in heaven forgive your trespasses.**

The Lord is not talking to sinners here; He's talking to believers — those who have the God-kind of faith. Sinners don't have the God-kind of faith. Only those who have been born again have received the God-kind of faith. Every believer has a measure of it. Every believer can make it grow by exercising it and feeding it on God's Word. This God-kind of faith is of the heart, not the head. But it will not work where there is unforgiveness.

A Balanced Diet for Your Spirit

Some people don't like to hear this kind of teaching. They want to live the way they want to live and enjoy everything the way they want to enjoy it.

In Second Timothy 4:3, the Apostle Paul warned that the day would come when people would heap to themselves teachers who would teach what the people wanted to hear because they had "itching ears."

We will discuss this more in a later chapter, but I want you to realize that there are a lot of other doctrines in the Word of God besides faith and healing.

I know people who would get up and walk out of church if the preacher started teaching on a topic such as unforgiveness. They would say, "Bless God, I'm not going to listen to anything but *faith!*" They won't endure sound doctrine.

Feeding on only one part of the Word of God will do you harm. You need a balanced diet for your spiritual man just like you do for your natural man.

When I was a youngster in elementary school, our teachers showed us drawings of a fellow who ate candy, ice cream, and other junk food all the time. He started out big and strong, but after awhile, he became weak and wasted. Our teachers were trying to teach us that if we ate just one kind of food, we'd either become weak, wasted, or fat.

The same is true with "eating" or feasting on the Word of God. If you don't eat a balanced diet, you will become imbalanced. And do you know what happens to imbalanced people? Most of the time they go "off the deep end."

By using common sense, we could save ourselves a lot of problems, but for some reason, when some people get saved and filled with the Holy Spirit, they throw all their natural knowledge out the window.

I make the following statement all the time at RHEMA: *The natural and the supernatural working together become an explosive force for God!* Either one by itself doesn't always do the job; it takes both working together.

Why Prayers Aren't Answered

Unforgiveness is the reason why many people do not ever fulfill their divine destiny! Unforgiveness is the reason why many people do not get answers to their prayers. Oh, they can quote the Scriptures; they can make all the right confessions; they can give you the twenty-five steps of faith. But if unforgiveness is working in their life, faith will not work in their life.

I have counseled such people. They say, "I just don't understand it. My faith won't work. I can't understand what's going on."

I start asking questions to find out something about them. I often find they know the Word. They can even quote it. Then I begin to check up in some other areas. I begin to ask them about their lifestyle to find out if they're living in any kind of open sin that is not in line with God's Word. When I ascertain that they're living a good, clean life, I say, "All right, since all these other areas are clear, there's only one area left: the area of unforgiveness and walking in love. Has anyone done something to you that you think shouldn't have been done?"

"Well, it's funny you should ask that," a RHEMA student once replied. "About two months ago, my roommate decided he wanted to move out. We had made a pact to live together for the entire school year, but he decided he wanted to live by himself.

"I could not afford to keep our apartment — it was really nice — and I had to move into a 'dump.' I just don't like it, because he didn't hold up his end of the bargain. He did me wrong!"

I said, "What do you mean, he did you wrong? Didn't he give you notice?"

"Oh, yes, he told me two months before the lease ran out on the apartment. But, still, we had agreed to live together for the entire school year."

I said, "But he stayed the length of the time you signed the lease for, and besides that, he gave you two months' notice."

"I don't care. That wasn't right. He didn't do me right. I had to move to another place, and it's too far from school."

I said, "I want to tell you something, fellow. You'd better forget about it right now. If you don't, you're going to get in trouble in every area of your life."

He replied, "Well, I'm going to tell *you* something — I'm *not* going to forget the way he treated me. He treated me like dirt!"

Eventually, we had to expel that young man from RHEMA Bible Training Center with less than a month of the school year to go. Because he got upset with his roommate and wouldn't forgive him, he gave place to the devil. He began to rebel against the rules, saying, "I don't see why they've got that rule. I don't have to obey that. I don't believe that's in line with God's Word."

Because RHEMA is training people for the ministry, we make it mandatory for men to wear dress slacks and regular shirts to school, not jeans and

T-shirts. This fellow started coming to school wearing jeans and T-shirts. He'd argue, "Well, I don't see why I can't wear jeans and T-shirts! I'm free."

The faculty member who dealt with him said, "The main reason you can't wear them is because that's one of the rules that's been established at RHEMA."

He said, "But I don't find that in the Bible."

The faculty member said, "I don't find in the Bible where it says you've got to have a driver's license to drive, either, but you go out and try to drive without one. Get stopped by a policeman and see what happens to you."

At the beginning of the school year, this young man had been a very good student who showed promise. Then, by holding that grudge, he allowed unforgiveness into his heart.

What happened to him? The devil got him completely confused, hoodwinked, and all messed up. He went completely "off the deep end," rebelling against everything. And it all started with unforgiveness.

Unclog Your Spirit

Do you know what happens when you start holding grudges? It's similar to what happens in the arteries of your heart when too much fat gets in. Fat starts collecting around the edges of the artery and restricting the flow of blood. Once it starts collecting, it builds up until no blood can flow at all.

In the spiritual realm, unforgiveness builds up the same way. It starts collecting in the channel of your spirit where the Spirit flows, and if you're not careful, it'll clog the channel. Soon nothing is flowing at all.

So what can you do if your spirit is clogged with unforgiveness? Get on your knees before God, take the knife of the Holy Spirit, and cut out all that unforgiveness. When you get rid of it, the flow can start again.

You see, it says in God's Word, *"And when ye stand praying, forgive. . . ."* Of course, you don't always have to go to the individual who has offended you. Sometimes, I have gone to an individual to settle a matter, because I felt it was necessary. Other times, when I stand praying, the Lord brings it to my remembrance that someone has wronged me and that I have not forgiven them. So I simply say, "Lord, I forgive that person. I ask You now to forgive me for harboring a grudge against him."

Once you start holding grudges in one area and give the devil one inch of ground, he'll start to take

over in other areas of your life, and he'll push you
into a corner and begin to dominate your life.

Now, as I said, I do get upset at times. Anyone
with any gumption gets upset occasionally. But the
Word of God says, *"Be ye angry, and sin not: let not
the sun go down upon your wrath: Neither give
place to the devil"* (Eph. 4:26,27).

There's a difference between getting upset and
holding a grudge. I didn't say you couldn't ever disagree with someone. But did you know you can disagree *agreeably?* There are certain things in the
Word of God that allow room for differences of
opinion, and not everyone is going to see eye-to-eye
on everything. We can disagree on certain issues.

However, I'm not going to hold a grudge against
someone because he doesn't believe the same way I
do. If he believes in being saved by the blood of the
Lord Jesus Christ, that's what counts. If he truly
believes in salvation and tries to live in line with
God's Word, that is grounds enough for me to fellowship with him.

Forgiveness in the Church

Most charismatic churches are made up of people who have come out of denominational churches,
and some are holding grudges against their former

denominations. As soon as someone mentions their former church, they bristle, "Bless God, they did me wrong. They taught unbelief. They had no right to kick me out. I didn't do anything wrong!"

Even if someone did do you wrong or taught you wrong, you can't hold a grudge if you expect God to use you. Let that be between God and that other person. Remember, you have a destiny to fulfill! Do not let yourself be cut off from the flow of God's Presence by holding a grudge.

Many churches have problems because people in the congregation hold grudges against each other. They sit out there in the congregation, feeling they have been wronged and, without realizing it, play right into the devil's hands.

They keep the power of God from being able to move effectively among the whole body of believers, because they're thinking, *I can sing better than her! I don't know why the pastor put her up there to lead worship. I have a better voice. Listen to that! She went flat on that note.*

Or, someone might say, "I wish the pastor would shut up. He's been preaching thirty-five minutes. He already said that three times — what's he saying it again for?"

Someone else might be saying, "I taught that Sunday school class last year. The pastor should have chosen me to be the leader. I'm better qualified!

If you're not careful, this kind of thing will build up resentment in you, and before you know it, you won't want to go to church.

Instead of getting upset, acting in unforgiveness, and giving an evil report, you should give a good report. You should say, "Well, praise God, the pastor must know what he is doing."

You should go to that person chosen to teach your former class and say, "I taught this class last year. I have a lot of notes and research that you're welcome to use if you would like."

That's acting in love. That's the way it should be, because then the enemy will have no room to get in. Then the power of God can move. Then your words won't snare you and keep you from fulfilling your divine destiny.

PROVERBS 6:2
**2   Thou art snared with the words of thy mouth,
thou art taken with the words of thy mouth.**

The Power of Words

The Book of James has a lot to say about this. James talks about the wagging tongue. He talks about having faith. And he poses the question of how faith is going to work if that tongue is always wagging!

(That is what's the matter with a lot of people. God couldn't move if He wanted to because they're never quiet long enough for Him to say anything to them.)

Words are containers. They are either filled with hate, doubt, and unbelief, or they are filled with love, joy, peace, faith, and goodness. You build an atmosphere with words.

It's the same in the spiritual realm: *Forgive and keep a good report.* Let whatever flows out of your mouth be good!

If you have all the "formulas" right, but your prayers are not getting answered, the first thing to do is check to see if you're holding a grudge against someone. Remember, there's nothing wrong with the *power* end (God), so the problem must be on the *receiving* end (you).

If you're tuning in to a radio station and the signal is garbled, you don't call the radio station and say, "Hey, your signal's no good; you need to check the transmitter."

No, it's usually not the fault of the transmitter; something is wrong with your radio. *You* have to do something. Either the tuner is not working properly, or you're too far away from the signal to receive it with the type of antenna you have.

So when your faith's not working for you, you'd better start "fine-tuning" at your end of the line!

Never permit anything said about you to remain in your memory. If you think on those barbs long enough, they will begin to affect you. The devil will jump on your shoulder and say, "If I were *you*, I'd wait for an opportunity to get back at that person!"

Many people have trouble like this on their jobs. They may feel that they've been wronged or passed over for promotions, so they try to get even with the person they believe wronged them. When they see that person make a mistake, they make sure the mistake is noticed by everyone.

That's harboring unforgiveness to the point that you begin to retaliate and sin against your fellow man.

Once as I was walking across the RHEMA campus, a young man came up to me and said, "I want you to forgive me."

I said, "What for?"

He said, "Don't you remember? The other day we were over at the recreation center and I said such-and-such."

I said, "No, I don't remember."

He said, "I do."

I said, "Well, now that you brought it up, I do recall your saying something to that effect. But I never hold anything against anyone. Yes, I forgive you."

I make it a rule that if someone says something against me, I forgive him at that very moment. And I never think of it again.

> **GALATIANS 6:1**
> 1   Brethren, if a man be overtaken in a fault, ye which are spiritual, restore such an one in the spirit of meekness; considering thyself, lest thou also be tempted.

Many people get into trouble when they see someone doing something *they* think is wrong (whether it is or not). They may say something like, "My goodness, I can't believe it! Look what he's doing. I don't believe that's right."

Even if it *is* wrong, Paul didn't say, "People, if a man be overtaken in a fault, you who are spiritual, get on the telephone and tell everybody about it."

Paul didn't tell you to say, "Do you know what I saw So-and-so doing? That isn't right. We ought to do something about that. We ought to go tell the pastor. We ought to bring it up before the church.

We ought to expose him." That's holding ought against your brother.

No, the Bible says, ". . . *ye which are spiritual, restore such an one in the spirit of meekness; considering thyself, lest thou also be tempted*" (Gal. 6:1).

When you stand praying, forgive those who have wronged you or others. Do not allow unforgiveness to get hold of you. I didn't say it would be easy, because sometimes it's not easy to forgive and forget.

Whenever I have trouble forgiving, I go back in my mind to Jerusalem, to Golgotha, a place by the garden outside the city walls. Many believe that is where Jesus hung on the Cross.

I remember the words He uttered as He was dying. He was stretched between Heaven and earth, the bridge on which man passes from sin to eternal life. He said, "Father, forgive them."

If the Son of God can forgive like that, then I can forgive too! When I find it hard to forgive and forget, I remember that Jesus forgave, and it becomes quite easy.

No one has put a crown of thorns on my head. No one has beaten my back bloody. No one has put me to death. Since Jesus forgave, so can I.

Our Helper

The Holy Spirit will help you forgive. *The Amplified Bible* quotes Jesus in John 14:16 as saying, "And I will ask the Father, and He will give you another Comforter (Counselor, Helper, Intercessor, Advocate, Strengthener, and Standby), that He may remain with you forever."

The Holy Spirit is a Helper. He is with you. If you choose to forgive and forget and to keep a good report, the Holy Spirit will help you. But until *you* choose to forgive, the Holy Spirit cannot help you. And oh, how He wants to help!

He wants to place a hand, as it were, over your mouth and say, "Don't say that! Don't think about that! Don't say that evil thing! Don't listen to that!" But the choice is yours.

It's your choice to speak faith words — loving words — and not to say anything evil. *You* control what comes out of your mouth. You can choose to talk about how badly you feel, how bad your circumstances are, or how badly someone acted toward you.

You can choose to talk about those in authority and bad-mouth them all day long, dwelling on their bad points. But if you dwell on these kinds of things, they will become a giant and "eat you alive."

On the other hand, you can choose to talk about God and how great He is. You can choose to say good things about people who have wronged you. You can choose to talk about the goodness of God, how great it is to be alive, and what a wonderful day God has made.

It's your choice whether to hold a grudge or to forgive.

It's your choice to speak faith words (positive words) or failure words (negative words).

If you choose to hold a grudge or to speak negative words, you will never fulfill your divine destiny. So choose to be positive and keep a good report. Refuse to hold ought against anyone. If someone wrongs you, just forget it — let it go — and pray for him or her.

True Forgiveness

Paul said in his writings, "Faith worketh by love" (Gal. 5:6). Love isn't bothered by trivial things. Love overlooks them. Love lets them go. Love forgives.

When you truly love someone, you forget his or her failings and mistakes. That's what the Word says God does with us. It says that when we repent for one sin, He forgives our sins and forgets them — it's as if we've never sinned.

When most people see their children doing something that they don't like, they correct them, but they don't continue to hold that mistake against them every time they make another. However, there are some people who dangle a previous mistake in front of a child, saying, "Remember what you did last week?" But, really, once you've corrected a problem and dealt with it, forget it and go on. Don't bring it back and hammer the child over the head with it.

A lot of people do that when it comes to forgiving someone. They may say they forgive, and they let the "offender" back into fellowship, but if that person steps out of line the least bit, they say, "Hey, remember what you did before? This is the second time I've had to talk to you about it!" How much forgiveness is in that?

Some people hinder their own prayers by reminding God of their past. He's forgotten it — He's forgiven you — so don't remind Him of it.

You see, *true forgiveness is acting like the sin or offense never happened.* That's true love — treating them the way you would if the wrong had never been committed.

If you want to be strong in faith, you've got to be strong in love and forgiveness. I realize that this is not an "exciting" teaching — it doesn't make you want to jump over pews or benches — but it will give you a foundation that will stand in the midst of life's storms.

I realize that many Christians have underlined all the verses in Mark 11 that we've read thus far, but you ought to doubly underscore where it says "And when ye stand praying, forgive . . ." (v. 25). That ought to be foremost in your heart and mind.

The person who wronged you has to answer to God. You don't answer for him or her; you answer for *you*. The only thing you can do for them is to forgive them, pray for them, and go on. You control you, not the other person.

Without forgiveness, it is impossible to make your faith work. And you need your faith to work in order to fulfill your destiny. If you want strong faith, learn how to forgive when you stand praying.

Chapter 8
Take Back What the Devil's Stolen

We have already said that *every* Christian has a divine destiny, and we have seen how the "past tense" of God's Word will reveal to us what that destiny is.

Then we can begin to lay the foundation for what we must do to make God's will for our lives a reality. The first thing I mentioned was learning to forgive. This will keep the channels open for the Presence of God to flow through our lives. This, as I said, is *foundational*. You see, you must have a solid foundation before you begin to build.

But now I want to share a few things with you about going on the "offensive." It's time for you to go out and *do* something! It's time for you to be on the *offensive* instead of always being on the *defensive*. It's time to take your future by force!

Recently, I began to think about the word "take," and I began to realize that things have to be *taken* in the spiritual ream. They don't just *fall* on you. You have to reach out and *take* them.

Salvation is an example. Did you get saved without reaching out and taking what God was offering you? Did salvation just fall on you? Or did you respond, reach out, and take the gift God was offering you in salvation?

How many businessmen attain success without going out and taking that success with diligence and hard work? Do they just sit back in their offices, put their feet up on their desks, and say, "Well, I'm a businessman. I know all the business principles," and have big business deals just fall on them? No, not often. They are successful because they go out, take hold of opportunities, and make them work.

It seems that man is programmed to be a success. Have you ever met someone who did not want to succeed? I've never met anyone who didn't want to succeed. Everyone I've ever met has wanted to be a success.

Some people may say they don't want to be a success, but don't just listen to their words. Watch their actions. Their actions prove they want to be a success, because they're out striving for it every day.

Success comes when an individual realizes what he has, who he is, and what abilities he possesses in the natural. Then he takes those abilities and surrounds himself with people who have abilities in the areas where he is weak. Together, they make a strong team so they can go out and take success.

Usually, if you study business partners closely, you will find that one has expertise in one area, and his partner has expertise in another area. Put them together, and they have expertise in all areas of their business. If they need more expertise, they'll go out and find department heads or supervisors to handle those jobs. And they become successful.

I'm talking about natural things here. I like to bring things down to where you can see the parallel between success in the natural realm and success in the spiritual realm.

Most people try to divorce the two, putting natural life in one corner and spiritual life in another. But the truth is: You are a *natural* human being. You live in a natural world. At the same time, however, you are a *spiritual* being — a spirit. You live in a spirit world. You must learn to combine the two with God and become an explosive force in both areas of your life.

Responding to God's Gifts

That's where the word "take" comes is. It's a small word, and when I say it, most people immediately get a visual impression in their minds.

(Whether you realize it or not, when you hear a word, it automatically triggers a "memory bank" in your brain, which brings up a certain definition or image of that word.)

When I hear the word "take," the image it triggers in my mind is a hand reaching out taking hold of something. What kind of mental picture do you get?

It doesn't matter which translation of the Bible you own — it still contains 32,000 promises made by God Himself. For whom did Jesus purchase these 32,000 promises? For God? For the angels? No, they don't need them. Jesus purchased them for His Church.

God gave us Jesus — all that He is, all that He has, and all that He has done. That's what has been given to the Church. Second Peter 1:3 says, *"According as his* [Jesus] *divine power hath given unto us all things that pertain unto life and godliness. . . ."* Notice the word "hath" in that scripture. Is "hath" past tense, present tense, or future tense? It's *past tense*!

If someone "hath" (or has) done something for you, it's yours. If God "hath" given unto us all things that pertain to life and godliness, how should we respond?

Suppose I'm away from home holding a service, and a delivery boy walks through the door of the church and says, "Telegram for you." I open that telegram, and it announces that the richest man in the world has put a million dollars into my bank account in Tulsa, Oklahoma. Everyone would praise God with me, wouldn't they?

But suppose the next day you accompany me to the airport, and I sit in the waiting room whining and complaining, "I sure would like to go back to Tulsa! I sure would like to go back home, but I haven't got a ticket."

You'd say, "Hey, I thought you had a million dollars down there in your bank account! You got that telegram while you were here. The money's yours."

"Oh, yes. I know that. I sure wish I could get home."

You'd think something was wrong with me if I did that! You would know that all I had to do was go to the counter and purchase a ticket, write out a check, or charge it — because I had the money in the bank to cover it.

Well, what is the difference between that and spiritual things? God *hath* already given us everything that pertaineth to life and godliness. Why are we sitting around whining, crying, and saying to one another, "I just don't know what is going to happen. I don't know if I'm going to be able to make it or not. The devil has been after me. My life is so torn up!"

That's what a lot of people are doing! I didn't say they aren't born again. I didn't say they aren't filled with the Spirit. They *have* already been given everything that pertains to life and godliness. They're just not *acting* on that fact. They're not acting as if it's so!

That's where the word "take" comes in. By faith, we reach out and *take* what belongs to us. So begin to live in the success, happiness and liberty of the power of the Word of God. *Faith takes it!*

Someone wrote that the word "receive" in Mark 11:24 could be translated "take with force" or "seize with a grip that cannot be shaken loose."

Receive what God has for you! How? By reaching up in faith and taking it! The problem is that most people are waiting for God to hover over them like a gardener over his flowers. They're waiting for God to stand over the top of them with a little watering pot. Then they'll get excited and say, "God just poured me out a blessing!"

No, God poured out a blessing on the Church some two thousand years ago when Jesus Christ

Himself, suspended between Heaven and earth on that rugged cross, said, "It is finished."

Jesus died, went into the pits of hell, and conquered the enemy. Then He rose victorious over death, hell, and the grave, ascended to Heaven, and sat down at the right hand of the Father. He purchased all there is in life and godliness — and He has given it to the Church.

We don't have to wait for God to come by and pour us out a blessing! All we have to do is know who we are in Christ, what we have in Christ, and reach up and take what belongs to us!

The Holy Spirit could say to us, as the angels said to those who were gazing heavenward after Jesus' ascension, ". . . *why stand ye gazing up into heaven? this same Jesus, which is taken up from you into heaven, shall so come in like manner as ye have seen him go into heaven*" (Acts 1:11).

As I mentioned in previous chapters, too often Christians are sitting here in this world, gazing off into the far blue yonder, looking for some kind of "pie in the sky," singing about the "Sweet By-and-By," or talking about how great it's going to be on the other side.

Heaven is going to be great — and I thank God for it — but I'm interested in what can help me in the right-here-and-now. *Now* is when I'm living. *Now* — not in the "Sweet-By-and-By" — is when I need something to carry me through any kind of crisis. Thank God for the promise of Heaven; I need that as inspiration to keep me going. But I need something to carry me right now in the face of the darkness of this world.

The Word of God gives me that "something," and it says that the blessings are mine if I will just *take* them!

Things That Shake Faith

If we go to the story of Peter walking on the water (Matt. 14), we find that once he stepped outside the boat, he really did begin to walk on the water. But what happened when Peter took his attention off of Jesus and the power of God? What happened when Peter began to look at a bank of waves on one side of him — and then saw another bank of waves on the other side?

As long as Peter kept his eyes on Jesus, he walked up and over the crest of those waves — but when the next wave looked as if it was going to break over him, Peter began to sink.

The same circumstances that caused Peter to sink are robbing modern Christians of their happiness and joy and keeping them from taking by faith what God has already given. Like Peter, we have begun to look, listen, and feel the power of the enemy. We have gotten our eyes off of God and the things of God. The waves of depression, sadness, sickness, disease, and short bank accounts have become a part of our life because our attention is misdirected.

The *first* thing that is robbing us is the things we *feel*. Peter *felt* the wind blowing on him. You can't see the wind, but you can feel the effects of it.

Second, Peter was affected by the things he *saw*. He *saw* the dark threatening waves. What kinds of things do we see in this era that shake our faith? We see television newscasts, newspapers, and magazines filled with reports of fear, doubt, unbelief, and depression.

But I want you to know that you can reach up by the hand of faith and take what belongs to you. You can begin to claim God's promises. You do not have to be swept under by depression over the crises of this world.

You may not know how God is going to do it, but in His Word He has promised that He shall supply *". . . all your need according to his riches in glory by Christ Jesus"* (Phil. 4:19).

In the summer of 1980, our ministry crusade team and I traveled from Oklahoma to California, up the West Coast of Canada, and then all the way across Canada. Someone asked me, "Aren't you afraid? They've been talking about a fuel shortage. What if you get your bus out there in the middle of the desert, and you can't buy gas?"

I replied, "God took care of the children of Israel. As long as they believed Him, they walked across the burning sand, and not one ounce of shoe leather was burned off the bottom of those sandals they were wearing. My God is the same God today. He's still the same Jehovah who carried the children of Israel. He is still *El Shaddai* — the God who is more than enough!

"And if He has to, He will *manufacture* diesel in that fuel tank — and we'll carry the Gospel of the Lord Jesus Christ. I am scheduling *more* crusades, as a matter of fact. I've alerted the crusade team to be ready for them."

You see, I am going to take what is rightfully mine. The Word of God says it's mine. I've read the Bible, and it tells me that these things belong to me, and I'm not about to let the devil steal what belongs to me.

No Trespassing!

Suppose you drove up to your house and found a moving van backed up to your door and men are busy moving all your belongings out of the house. You would ask, "What is going on here?"

Suppose a man walked up to you and said, "Here's the deed. This says that the house belongs to me, and I'm moving in. I've sold all your furniture, and I'm moving it out. I'm going to be moving my furniture in and living here."

You wouldn't walk back to your car and say to your wife, "Well, honey, I thought that this was our house, but that man has a piece of paper that says it belongs to him. I don't know how it happened, but I guess it belongs to him, so we might as well go down to Aunt Mary's and see if they'll let us spend the night until I can figure out what to do."

No, you wouldn't do that! You would go to the proper authorities and find out what was going on. You would demand your rights, because you know that house belongs to you. Yet, as the Church of the Lord Jesus Christ, what do we often do when the devil comes by, backs up his moving van, and tries to steal our joy while moving in his sickness and disease?

We say, "Well, I *thought* the Lord was going to take care of me, but I guess He isn't." That's what is the matter with us; we are allowing the devil to rob us needlessly. God already *has* given us *all* things that pertain unto life and godliness.

Second Peter 1:3 says that all of us can live in happiness. It says that all of us can live in prosperity. It says that all of us can live in health. It says that all of us can have spiritual authority. It says that all of us have become joint-heirs with Jesus Christ. We are the sons of God!

When the devil backs his moving van up to my property, I look him square in the eye and say, "Hey — didn't you see that 'no trespassing' sign out there? Get your moving van out of here! Pack up your goods, Mr. Devil. You have no right and no authority to come in and steal my happiness, health, joy, finances, and prosperity. I have taken them by faith. God said they are mine. You have no right and no authority to them!"

That's what you would tell someone if he backed a moving van up to your house unbidden. You would say, "This is mine. You have no authority — you have no rights — here." And you would run him off your property.

Well, do the same thing with the Word of God when the devil comes to steal what belongs to you! Take the Word of God and say, "It is written, Mr. Devil" and quote scriptures to him.

That reminds me of a story I heard my dad tell. He said it came from Smith Wigglesworth.

A woman left her house one day and started walking down the street to wait for a bus. Her little old dog followed her. The woman looked at the dog and said, "Now, honey, you can't go today. Go back to the house."

The little old dog didn't pay any attention. It just wagged its tail more and kept trotting right behind her.

The woman stopped again, looked back, and said, "Now, honey, you can't go today. Go on back to the house."

She proceeded on down the street and waited at the corner for the bus. That little old dog just walked around her, his tail flopping, licking her on the feet and sitting there, panting, looking up at her, like little dogs do.

By this time, the bus was coming down the street. The woman looked at the dog and said, "Go! Get back to the house!" When she said that, that little dog tucked its tail between its legs and — zoom —it ran back to that house in a hurry.

Smith Wigglesworth said, "That's the way you have to deal with the devil. He'll take all that 'honey' business you want to give him. But if you really mean business, take the Word of God and say, 'It is written. Get out of here, devil! I resist you in the Name of Jesus!' And you will get results."

Handling Contradictory Thoughts

We must quickly cast away every thought that is contrary to the Word of God. No, you can't keep a bird from flying over your head, but you certainly can keep it from building a nest in your hair!

When you walk this walk of faith and learn to take things by faith, you can't keep the devil from bringing his contradictory thoughts and contradictory circumstances for you to see — but you can refuse to think on them.

You can combat the devil's devices by quoting, "It is written. I take what belongs to me, Mr. Devil, because the Word says that no weapon formed against me will prosper (Isa. 54:17). The Word says, Mr. Devil, that my body is healed by the power of God. It is written, Mr. Devil, that my every need is met."

We have more than 17,000 RHEMA Bible Training Center graduates living and ministering around the world today. Our more than 100-acre campus has several million dollars' worth of improvements and buildings on it. All of that didn't happen by my sitting around my office saying,

"Well, I guess if the Lord wants us to have the blessings, He will give them to us."

No, those things happened by Brother Hagin, myself, and a lot of other people taking the Word of God and delivering it in the devil's face — in the face of hindrances, obstacles, and adverse circumstances.

Once, the ministry was caught in a terrible cash flow crunch. If I had listened to the enemy, who had begun to camp on my shoulder and talk in my ear, I still would be hiding under my desk, afraid to stick my head out. I listened to that old boy about all I could, and then I jumped to my feet and said, "Mr. Devil, get out of here! Get out of my office! It is written! I take what God has promised me! I take it by faith!"

And he would reply, "But where is the money coming from?"

I would answer, "I don't know where it's coming from. That's not my part of the contract. My part of the contract is to believe God. It's God's part to make it come true. And the Word of God says that He never fails. He never has failed yet, and He's not going to fail me now. So, Mr. Devil, get out of here!"

When you resist the devil, he will take off for a while, but he won't stay gone long. He will come back, battering at the same door. If you don't keep reinforcing that door with the faith that takes, he eventually will batter it down. And if he ever batters it down and gets his foot in the door, you are in trouble. *The best way to combat the devil is not to let him get a foothold in the first place!*

For example, how many of you have ever awakened with a little scratching sensation in your throat? The tendency is to ignore it, hoping it will go away. But by the end of the day, if you haven't dealt with it, the thing will have hold of you. It is harder to get your healing then, after something has hold of you, than it is in the morning when you have that first symptom.

So grab the Word of God and run the enemy away before he ever starts unpacking. (It's always easier to move someone out *before* he unpacks!)

Take your answer by faith. Symptoms may linger, but don't pay any attention to the symptoms. Stay focussed on God and His Word.

In Mark 11:13,14 the fig tree was dead when Jesus cursed it, even though its leaves were still waving green in the breeze. It wasn't until twenty-four hours later that those leaves turned brown and the disciples noticed that the tree had died. But the tree *actually* died when Jesus cursed it.

The minute you first reach out by faith and take hold of that sickness, disease, or whatever is binding you, and command it to turn loose, it becomes a reality in the spirit world. And by constantly holding fast to your confession, you can take what is already a reality in the spirit world and bring it into reality in the natural, physical world in which you live.

The thing that stops most people when they reach out and take hold of what they need by faith is that their grasp is weak. Remember, God already has given you 32,000 promises. He *hath* already given you all that pertains to life and godliness. What you must do by faith to receive these promises is reach out and grab them with a grip that can't be shaken by the least wind, wave, or any other contradictory circumstance. Hold onto these promises with the firm grip of steadfast faith in God!

Yes, you may feel like your situation is holding you rather than you holding it, but keep confessing God's Word. Say, "I've taken it by faith. It belongs to me. The Word says so."

Soon you will have what you are believing God for. The contradictory circumstances will be gone, and you'll be walking on to another victory. Then you'll reach out by faith and grab hold of something else, and you'll conquer it. Soon you'll reach

out and grab something else and conquer it too.
And you'll keep walking, confessing, and climbing
spiritually.

No, there is never a plateau. You will continue
to climb until the day Jesus Christ splits the clouds
of glory and takes us out of this world. There
should be a continual taking by faith and living by
faith in the awesome power of God.

This happiness — this abundant life — belongs
to you. Take it by faith. It is yours today. It is up to
you, not God, whether or not it becomes a reality in
your life. If you will do your part, God will see you
through.

God has said in His Word that He *hath* given us
all things that pertain to life and godliness. That
means *all* things. And Psalm 103:3 says that He
healeth *all* our diseases, not *part* of them.

Did God say in His Word that He would meet
our most important, pressing needs, but that we
would have to meet our little needs ourselves? Or
did He say He would meet *all* of our needs? He said
He would meet *all* of them (Phil. 4:19).

God is reaching His hand down from Heaven,
saying, "My child, here's all you ever need to have
happiness, godliness, and a joyous life on earth.
Here it is!"

You can look at that hand and say, "Oh, yes, I wish that were so. Oh, wouldn't that be nice!" Or you can, by faith, reach up and grab hold of all the provisions of life God's hand is offering you. *Never release your hold on God as He reaches down and offers the provisions of life to you.*

With your other hand, grab hold of the things that hinder you from enjoying these provisions and fling them from you. Your faith will activate God's power, and that power will flow through you to set you free from those hindrances.

You see, whether or not we receive the promises of God has a lot to do with us. God's not going to come hit you over the head with a twenty-pound sledgehammer and say, "Son, get in line. Here it is. Take it." He's not going to drop it on you. He's not going to spoon-feed you and force it down your mouth. No, all He's going to do is offer it. It's there for you to take.

You receive God's blessings with the faith that takes!

And after faith takes, *faith never turns loose!* And because faith never turns loose, it leads to success by the power of God.

Begin to talk to God. Whatever it is you need, tell Him what scriptures you're standing on.

If it's finances, quote scriptures about finances. If it's healing you need, quote scriptures about healing. Remind Him that He "hath" given to you all that pertains to life and godliness.

Tell Him that you are taking by faith what belongs to you and that you will never again relinquish what belongs to you in the Name of Jesus.

Because He *hath* purchased for us *all* that pertains to life and godliness, we can now reach up by the power of the Word of God and take what belongs to us. We can walk in victory in Christ Jesus.

Faith Rejoices Now!

Faith rejoices now — not when you see a manifestation of what you're believing for.

In one of my dad's meetings years ago, a little old man went down to the altar one Sunday and claimed his wife's salvation. After he claimed it by faith, he had a great Pentecostal time — a hilarious time — like the joyous time they had on the Day of Pentecost. You see, by faith, he took the answer *when he prayed.*

A few days, later, his wife attended church with him, went to the altar, and received her salvation.

That night, her husband sat in the back of the church with his arms folded, just looking at her.

The other church members, because they had been praying for her for a long time, were ecstatic.

Someone finally asked her husband, "Aren't you excited? That's your wife down there."

He replied, "Remember the other night when I got excited? I accepted it by faith then. I saw it then. So it's 'old news' now. Why should I get excited about it now? It already *happened* a week ago."

That's what faith does. *Faith rejoices at the moment of taking.* Faith doesn't rejoice when it sees a manifestation, because it's "old news" then.

Do what you would do if you saw what you were believing for happen this very moment — if you saw it take place in front of your eyes at this moment.

As you walk this great walk of faith, never again say, "I don't know if I'm going to make it or not."

From now on, talk in faith and take it by faith. Your circumstances may look bleak, but never relinquish your hold. Once you start out in faith, hold fast to your confession and praise God all the way to victory. Keep taking. Keep conquering the enemy. Keep winning more people to Jesus.

Take it by faith. Rejoice because you have everything that pertains to life and godliness. It is yours. Live like it — rejoice in it — and have a good time on the way to fulfilling your divine destiny!

Chapter 9
Build Strong Faith

We know that if we want to accomplish God's plan for our life, we must take possession of all that God has provided for us. As I said in the previous chapter, we take hold of God's provisions with the "hand of faith."

Only strong faith will triumph over every situation and circumstance. It is strong faith that takes back what the devil's stolen. And it is strong faith that turns your *destiny* into *reality*.

Many earnest Christians are asking the question: "How can I build strong faith?"

These people realize that the things they need from God — healing, prosperity, and other blessings — do not come simply because they have been born again. These blessings come through faith.

They realize that faith is not just an act of the will of man; faith is acting on God's Word.

But many do not know how to secure faith for the things they need from God. In this chapter, I will give you a formula to build strong faith for whatever you need from God.

The faith I'm talking about does not come from an act of the will. You can will something all you want — you can try to make it happen all you want — but it's not going to work that way. Faith is not designed that way. Here are some biblical principles to help you build the kind of faith you need in order to fulfill your divine destiny and possess all that God has provided for you.

First: To Build Strong Faith, Surround Yourself With That Which Produces Faith

Every Christian has received "the" measure of faith as mentioned in Romans 12:3. Not *a* measure of faith; it's *the* measure of faith.

> **ROMANS 12:3**
> **3   For I say, through the grace given unto me, to every man that is among you, not to think of himself more highly than he ought to think; but to think soberly, according as God hath dealt to every man the MEASURE of faith.**

What you do with your measure of faith after salvation is up to you — and what you do with it determines whether or not you grow in faith.

It's strange to me how many Christians surround themselves with things that cause them to be weak in faith. They sit in a church that does not teach the Word of God, listening to someone tell them that it's not God's will to heal, that it's God's will for them to be poor, and so forth. They try to stay spiritually alive in that negative atmosphere where people do not believe in the supernatural power of God.

God's Word says, ". . . *without faith it is impossible to please him* [God] . . ." (Heb. 11:6). We must realize that if we are going to nurture our faith — if we're going to build it into something that will produce results for us — we must surround ourselves with successful people of God, not negative people. And we must feed our minds and spirits on material that will build faith, not destroy it.

We don't feed faith by reading a steady diet of secular magazines or viewing a steady diet of secular television.

Turn off your television. Read your Bible and listen to good teaching tapes and good Christian music. Surround yourself with things of God — things that will nurture your faith. Listen to people strong in faith — any of the great teachers today. (Just be sure they are teaching you in line with God's Word.)

I'm not saying there's anything wrong with watching television. I've got a television in my home. Bless God, if I haven't got anything else to do — if I'm prayed up, if I don't have to go preach anywhere — and the Dallas Cowboys are playing, I'm going to be watching them!

Another one of my pastimes is reading western stories. I have found one author in particular that I enjoy. Over the years, I have read dozens of his books and they are just good western writing — no bad situations or language at all. I don't do a lot of this kind of reading, but I do a little of it, because I enjoy it. I enjoy life. God expects us to have some leisure time and to enjoy our leisure time, but we've got to put God and the things of God first.

The Faith Walk Is Balanced

I'm not talking about getting out of balance. A lot of "religious" people are so far over in the ditch in some areas that they are out of balance with life. Then the devil can get them off on tangents and into wrong doctrine.

The faith walk is balanced. Jesus grew in *all* areas of life — emotional, physical, spiritual, and social. We also need to learn to have God in all areas of our lives to become well-balanced people.

If you want to have strong faith, surround yourself with the things of faith. Don't live in the negative.

Some, however, live in the negative all the time. If you were to phone them and ask, "How are things going today?" they probably would reply: "Oh, I tell you, this is the worst day I've ever seen! I can hardly walk because the corn on my foot is hurting so badly. And I know the weather is going to change, because that old knee of mine is giving me a fit. The dog got run over yesterday, and rabbits got into my garden last night and ate everything. Joe called from work a while ago, and he almost cut his finger off. Got it caught in the machine."

How are you going to keep the supernatural power of God flowing in your life if you're surrounded by people who have a form of godliness but no supernatural power? This kind of situation will drain you like a battery, because nothing is being put into your spirit to charge it up.

You won't be able to get yourself "started," much less help someone else out of their troubles.

Let me share a little secret with you: The disciples didn't start their ministry with impressive faith. They were astonished at the things Christ did. When they tried their wings, they didn't do too well.

The disciples had walked with Jesus; they were surrounded by that faith atmosphere for a few short years of His earthly ministry. They had been with Jesus when He calmed the storm, and they had marvelled, saying, "... *What manner of man is this* ... *?"* (Mark 4:41).

They had seen faith in action as Jesus spoke something and it happened. They had lived in Jesus' atmosphere of victory and faith. They had been filled with the Holy Spirit on the Day of Pentecost.

In Acts 4, we see the disciples again. The same Pharisees, scribes, and chief priests who had known them as weak disciples of Jesus looked at them now and realized that they had been somewhere special? Where? Down at the synagogue? No. Down at the Temple? No.

> **ACTS 4:13**
> 13 . . . when they saw the boldness of Peter and John, perceived that they were unlearned and ignorant men, they marvelled; and they took knowledge of them, that THEY HAD BEEN WITH JESUS.

What did the religious leaders see? They saw "unlearned and ignorant men" doing the same things Jesus had done. They saw the same miracles being performed. They saw the same atmosphere surrounding Peter, John, and the others that had surrounded Jesus Christ.

They witnessed the same words and the same power. And they knew that these simple men did not receive it any other way except from being in the atmosphere where teaching and miracles were taking place.

It had become a part of their innermost beings. When the disciples went out to minister it was the same as Jesus ministering!

You and I live in an age where people should be taking notice that we have been with Jesus! He was the *Living* Word to those disciples in the first century. He is the *written* Word to us, the disciples of today.

Do you want to work for God? Do you want to move with God? Fellowship with people who believe as you do and with people who teach faith. Surround yourself with the Word of God and with that which produces strong faith.

Second: To Build Strong Faith, Build On the Word of God, Not Experience

As I was praying for someone in a service once, a woman came running up, exclaiming, "Oh, I had that same thing! Let me tell you about my experience. It will probably help him!"

I said, "No, I don't want you to tell him your experience."

Why? Because God doesn't always move the same way all the time. Too many people have put God in a little box, so to speak, and they believe He only moves in the confines of that box. If He doesn't move just exactly the way they think He should, they don't believe it is of God. But you can't lock God and the power of the Holy Spirit in a box!

Don't try to make people receive salvation, the baptism of the Holy Spirit, or healing the way you feel they should be received or the way you experienced it.

I've known people who received the baptism of the Holy Spirit while seated in a circle with other people. Then they think that everyone must receive just as they did — sitting in a chair in that circle! Now it can certainly happen that way, but it doesn't *have* to. Sitting in a chair in a circle of people doesn't have a thing to do with receiving the Holy Spirit.

Other people have said to me, "Brother, I've dealt with demons, and let me tell you my experience — the way I dealt with them. If you'll deal with them like I do, you'll have more success at casting out demons."

But, no, that's not necessarily true. The *Word of God* tells me how to deal with demons. I'm not interested in hearing someone's experiences of how he dealt with the devil. God may deal with me differently about handling a certain situation, or I can handle it according to the Word of God.

Every devil in hell is afraid of the Name of Jesus. Jesus has already defeated the devil and demons, so you do not need to come against them with anything but Jesus' Name. All you have to do is know who you are in Jesus, speak the Word — and the devil's got to go! It doesn't take three weeks. You'll understand that if you study what the Bible has to say about this subject.

Do you want to be spiritual? Do you want to get in on the move of God? Do you want to develop in and walk in faith? Then build on God's Word. Notice that Jesus didn't build on experience. He taught the Word. When he withstood Satan's temptations, He kept saying, "It is written, it is written, it is written."

Third: To Build Strong Faith, Look to the Word of God, Not Someone's Personality

If you're going to have strong faith to receive from God, build it on the Word, not on someone's personality.

Have you ever watched Brother Hagin preach? He doesn't put too much of his personality into it.

He keeps his personality suppressed so people will look at what the Word says.

The Bible says, *"He sent his word, and healed them, and delivered them from their destructions"* (Ps. 107:20). God didn't send a personality. He sent His Word. Forget about personalities.

God Has No Second Best

Many people come to Tulsa, Oklahoma, and say, "We came down here for Brother Hagin to pray for us."

Sometimes we have to tell them, "He's not in town," or "He has shut himself away for a time of prayer, fasting, and study." We add, "Someone else will be glad to minster healing to you. We've got all our RHEMA instructors here. We've got all kinds of personnel. Any one of them could lay hands on you and pray for you."

"No," they say. "We want Brother Hagin. We don't want second best."

I tell them, "There is no second best with God. Healing does not have to come from a certain man laying hands on you."

"That's all right," they say. "We'll just go over to Oral Roberts!"

Then if someone tells them that Brother Roberts is not in town, they'll say, "Well, we'll just go over to Kenneth Copeland. *He'll* pray for us."

You see, people begin looking to personalities instead of the Word of God. But a person is not going to heal them. It's the Word of God that's going to heal them. And the Word of God says, referring to any believer, "*. . . they shall lay their hands on the sick, and they shall recover*" (Mark 16:18).

That means a little child could lay hands on you and pray for your healing. And if you would believe as God's Word says, you could be healed from a child's prayers just as easily as you could from an adult's or a preacher's prayers. The Bible does not even require someone who is specially anointed to pray for healing. It just says "*. . . them that believe . . .*" (Mark 16:17). *If you're a believer, you qualify to lay hands on the sick!*

When people come to me and say, "My faith is weak, and I need healing," I suggest they go through the Word of God and meditate on and memorize scriptures concerning healing.

They say, "Well, that will take a lot of time."

I reply, "You'll find that Brother Hagin already has put those scriptures together in a minibook called *God's Medicine*. Get that book out every time you think of it in the next two weeks and begin to quote those scriptures out loud. Read them until they become a part of your innermost being. Build the Word inside of you."

I have seen those same people later, and they've said, "Do you know what? I did not even have to go forward to be prayed for! I just started walking in the light of the Word of God, and my sickness disappeared instantly." You see, the Word can do it.

God has given us many different ways to receive healing from Him. One is through prayer by the laying on of hands. Another is by the prayer of agreement. But the highest and most rewarding way is to receive on your own faith in line with God's Word. Walking in perfect harmony and unity with God — just you and God — is the highest kind of faith.

You need to know what the Word of God says so that when symptoms, financial peril, or disaster strikes, you can compete in the arena of faith.

If you know what God's Word says, every time Satan starts to take a swing at you, you can say, "It is written . . ." and block it. When he comes at you with another weapon, you can say, "It is written . . ." and that same shield of faith is lifted, blocking all of the enemy's darts.

Fourth: To Build Strong Faith, Obedience Is Necessary

Just knowing what the Word of God says won't be enough to defeat the enemy if you're not walking in the light of that Word. You must also be obedient — knowing what God's Word says to do and *doing it!*

> **1 JOHN 3:22**
> **22 And whatsoever we ask, we receive of him** [God], **because WE KEEP HIS COMMANDMENTS, AND DO THOSE THINGS THAT ARE PLEASING IN HIS SIGHT.**

> **JOHN 15:7**
> **7 If ye abide in me** [Jesus]**, and my words abide in you, ye shall ask what ye will, and it shall be done unto you.**

Notice the connection between these scriptures. In First John, the apostle wrote, ". . . *whatsoever we ask, we receive of him, BECAUSE we keep his commandments. . . .*" We cannot keep His commandments, however, unless we know what the Word of God says — unless His Word abides in us.

John also said, *"Beloved, if our heart condemn us not, then have we confidence toward God"* (1 John 3:21).

How are we confident? We are confident if our hearts don't condemn us. We have confidence toward God that He will do exactly what He has said.

God does not require us to walk in the light of some archangel. God does not require us to walk in the light of some man's doctrine. God does not require us to walk in the light of church tradition. God does not require us to walk in the light of a denomination.

God *does* require us to walk in the light of the eternal Word of God. That's what we're required to be obedient to.

When we walk in the light of this Word, *then* we can have confidence and know that what God said He will perform, He will do; *then* we have the right to claim what is ours.

If we continuously do not do what is right in the sight of God, and do not live the way we should, there is no way we can have confidence that God is going to give us what He said we could have.

It's not that He won't; He can't, because we're not walking in line with His Word.

It doesn't matter how much God wants to bless us — and He wants to minister to every one of us — He cannot bless us if we are not living right, because God cannot condone sin. Blessing us while we are living in sin would imply that His stamp of approval is on what we are doing, and it cannot be.

Many people are going around making faith confessions that are never going to come true. These confessions are never going to come true because the people are not living in line with God's Word.

There is a right way to live in line with God's Word, and it doesn't have to do with a set of rules — dos and don't's — either. It is obedience to the Word of God and to His Spirit.

When we are obedient, we have the right to claim what is ours as children of God.

Fifth: To Build Strong Faith, You Must Have Humility

A lot of people are proud of their humility! I've met a lot of people who brag that they are "faith people." Their attitude is, "If you're not where *we're* at, you haven't got it, brother."

As far as I'm concerned, this is a sectarian point of view. It is not biblical.

The disciples had this same attitude in Luke 9. They got prideful and puffed up. But when a child was brought to them, they couldn't cast the tough, stubborn, unclean spirit out of him (v. 40).

Jesus explained to the disciples that this kind comes out only by prayer and fasting.

They lacked humility and discipline. This hindered their faith.

The disciples had not been able to understand Christ's conversation regarding His imminent death on the Cross. They were looking for the Kingdom of God to be set up on earth then and there. And as we read further in Luke, we see other reasons why the disciples could not perform this great miracle.

They began to discuss their own importance (v. 46). They began to argue over who was going to sit where in the coming Kingdom! They even asked the Lord about it: "Can I sit here, Lord?" They were building themselves up. "Look who we are! We're someone!"

They even began to talk about who was *greatest* in the Kingdom! Notice their spiritual poverty in the following verses:

LUKE 9:49,50
49 And John answered and said, Master, we saw one casting out devils in thy name; and we forbad him, because he followeth not with us.
50 And Jesus said unto him, Forbid him not: for he that is not against us is for us.

So we see a sectarian spirit rising among the disciples. "Hey — you're not with us!" they said. "You quit that! You're not part of our little group." But Jesus said, ". . . *Forbid him not: for he that is not against us is for us*".

Notice something else. Immediately after this, we find the disciples accompanying Jesus into a town that would receive neither Him nor His message.

When James and John saw this, they were furious. They asked hopefully, ". . . *Lord, wilt thou that we command fire to come down from heaven, and consume them, even as Elias did?*" (v. 54).

Jesus immediately rebuked this kind of spirit. He told the disciples, ". . . *the Son of man is not come to destroy men's lies, but to save them . . .*" (v. 56).

Some people have thought that they have a monopoly on the gifts of God. The devil has used this kind of thinking to destroy, divide, and split apart the real move of the power of God.

We need to be humble before God — but I'm not talking about being a doormat. I'm talking about realizing that we would not be where we are today without the grace and love of God.

Sometimes we preachers get the idea that if people aren't ministered to under our ministry, they aren't going to get helped. But sometimes it's lay people, not ministers, who promote this idea. Lay people can be partly responsible for ministers' getting lifted up in pride when they have favorite ministers and won't allow anyone else but their favorites to pray for them or minister to them.

So you see, if we're not careful, we can lift up other people to the point they think they're someone. We believers are someone with the power of God — but we're *nothing* without it.

Saying we are children of God is vastly different from sticking your thumbs under your lapels and boasting, "Bless God, I'm a man of *faith* and *power*! If you're having to take any medicine or go to any doctor — you're sinning! You're not believing God."

The man who says that is a liar. Yes, there is a better way than going to a doctor and taking medicine, but you're not sinning if you do these things. You can believe God *and* go to the doctor!

I want to tell you something — if you don't have enough faith to be healed, you should get to a doctor and get some medicine to keep you alive long enough to get pumped full of the Word of God so you can believe God and walk away *healed*!

There are other subjects besides healings that Christians argue about which has caused strife and division and kept some people from receiving any part of the Gospel.

For example, how many more people would be free today if someone hadn't stood on their soapbox and said, "Hey, don't have anything to do with those people over there, because they don't wear our denominational hat." And how many more people would be in the Kingdom of God today if some Christians had not been so hard on those who understood the New Birth but just didn't understand the infilling of the Holy Spirit.

You're going to see people in Heaven, and you're going to wonder how they got there, because they didn't come out of *your* mold. But there's only one mold they must come out of. They must know Jesus Christ as their personal Savior, and they must live a godly kind of life according to the Word of God.

Yes, I believe everyone should go on to the next step and receive the infilling of the Holy Spirit and all God has for them. But if they accept Jesus Christ and live a godly life, they're just as saved as you or I, praise God.

Let's get away from our sectarian thinking. We need to have some humility. We all live down here on this earth together, and we need to live peaceably, not in strife and division.

I guarantee you, if we live in line with God's Word, we can build a faith that can bring part of Heaven down here while we're on earth. I'll tell you why: All that is in Heaven belongs to us — all of it is ours — because we have become heirs of the promise.

There is no monopoly on the power of God. One group *does not* have it monopolized. I can tell you what group does have it monopolized — the group of the blood-bought, born-again Church of the Lord Jesus Christ!

I'm not talking about *a* church — I'm talking about *the* Church, called in Greek the *ecclesia*, the "called-out ones."

Sixth: To Build Strong Faith, You Must Have Holy Boldness

This is something many people need badly. Most people are afraid of the devil. They would rather hide from him than to stand against him.

But you're going to have to be able to boldly claim what belongs to you in the Name of El Shaddai, the God who is more than enough.

You're going to have to be willing to stand, look the devil square in the eye, and say, "You hoodwinked me and fooled me for the last time! Either get out of the way, or get ready to get run over!"

Bless God, I'm not afraid to face the devil. In fact, if I see him about fifty yards down the street, I call, "Hey! Devil! I'm talking to *you!*" He ducks around a corner. He doesn't want any part of me.

He doesn't want any part of an individual who knows who he is in Jesus Christ, because Jesus defeated Satan. He knows that an informed Christian is going to start speaking that Word with his mouth. And every time those words come out of his mouth, it's like someone hitting him with a whip. He doesn't want any part of a believer who knows his place in Christ.

Yet the Church has been so beaten down — so cowed down — that its members are not bold anymore. Instead of going out *looking* for the devil, they hide if they see him coming. I really believe that some people have more reverence for the devil than they have for God. When they start talking about the devil, they get *quiet.*

Brother Hagin tells about being in California in 1950 in the middle of a flu epidemic. Everything was shut down. Some preachers were standing around talking with the pastor after church.

They said, "Do you think you're going to have to shut this meeting down?"

The pastor replied, "No, Brother Hagin won't let me shut it down because of the epidemic."

One of the preachers said, "Well, aren't you afraid you'll all get the flu? Man, you're down to almost no people in attendance. There were hardly fifty people here tonight. I had an evangelist over at my church. He closed the meeting down to go home and get ready to have the flu. Said he felt it coming on."

About that time, my dad walked up.

They said, "Brother Hagin, aren't you afraid you're going to have the flu?" (They said it quietly.)

"No," he said. "And I'll tell you something. I'm not *ever* going to have the flu."

"Oh, Brother Hagin!" one man whispered. "I wouldn't say that if I were you! The *devil* will hear you!"

Dad just reared back and said loudly, "Yes, that's the very dude I *want* to hear me!

"I want him to know that I know who I am in Christ Jesus; I want him to know that I know what I have because of what Jesus has done for me and that he's not fooling with some novice who doesn't know what he is doing.

"I want him to know he's not going to run over me.

"I want him to know it now, so I don't have to have a fight later on."

You've got to have holy boldness. You've got to be willing to be in the forefront of the battle.

Young people at a church where I once was associate pastor used to say, "Ken, you pray funny."

I would ask, "What do you mean?"

They said, "When you pray, it's just like you were talking to your daddy."

I said, "I am. I'm talking to my Heavenly Father."

I don't have to crawl to God on my hands and knees and beg and plead anymore than I have to crawl into my dad's office in Tulsa and beg and plead with him.

I walk in there boldly. If his door is shut, I knock, open it, and walk in. Why? Because he's my father. I'm his son. I have the privilege of being in there. You think about that!

When my daughter, Denise, was little and visited our offices, it didn't matter to her if my office door was closed. She would come popping through that door. That was her daddy's office!

She would also go bouncing through every closed door into Dad's, her Pa-Pa's, office. There could be ten people sitting in his office, but she would go straight to her grandfather and climb up on his knee. Why? Because that was her right and privilege. She was part of the family, an heir of the family.

Be Bold!

I want to tell you something: We are joint-heirs with Jesus Christ. We have a right to be bold about our position. We must learn to walk in that position. We must learn to walk in that boldness — *even when we're hurting* — proclaiming God's Word.

Boldly take whatever you need from God. Boldly proclaim it. Grab hold of it with the tenacity of a bulldog that grabs hold of a bone and won't turn it loose.

I grabbed hold of this Word many years ago. I'll never relinquish my hold on the Word of God. I'll walk through life victoriously because this kind of faith belongs to me. I'm going to walk in the light of God's Word, quote God's Word, and be what I'm supposed to be in the Kingdom of God. I am going to fulfill my divine destiny. And you can, too, if you want to.

Boldly, authoritatively proclaim your deliverance in the areas of finances, healing, habits, or whatever. The words spoken by your mouth are a creative force. It is your mouth that will turn the power of God loose for you as you quote His Word.

Boldly begin to proclaim what is yours according to the Word of God. Think of a scripture that covers your particular situation. Stand on that scripture. Boldly proclaim and quote that scripture verse.

If you need finances, boldly proclaim to ministering spirits (angels) to cause finances to come to you. Boldly say (and say it loudly), "Devil, take your hands off my finances! You have no authority and no right."

If you need deliverance from a habit, begin to command that you are free according to the Word of God, because "greater is He that is in you, than he that is in the world" (1 John 4:4). The Greater One has delivered you and set you free. Right now you are going on record that you already have been delivered, and you're proclaiming that deliverance now. Be bold. Put your voice to it.

Be authoritative in the way you deal with the devil. As long as you are mealy-mouthed, he's going to keep hanging around, doing what he's been doing.

But if you open your mouth and speak with authority — backed by the Word of God — he's going to turn and run, because the Word of God says, *". . . Resist the devil, and he will flee from you"* (James 4:7). Get what belongs to you!

Confession:

It is done.

It is done.

It is done.

Because the Word of God says it,

I will not be moved by what I feel;

I will not be moved by what I see.

I will only be moved by what God's Word says.

I am delivered.

I am free in Jesus Christ.

Chapter 10
Live a Life of Love

We have seen that we need strong faith to fulfill our divine destiny. That's the kind of faith that takes back what the devil has stolen and takes rightful possession of all that belongs to us in Christ Jesus. We have also learned how to build the strong faith we need. Now let's look at some pitfalls to faith.

We must be able to recognize pitfalls if we want to learn how to avoid them. And it's *vital* that we avoid every pitfall in order to keep our faith working. You see, without faith, we will never fulfill our divine destiny and possess all that God has provided for us.

The Lord gave me something as I was praying and asking Him questions about so-called "faith" people who weren't getting answers to their prayers.

He told me that people who know the faith message today are not missing it in their confessions.

They are not missing it in knowing what the Word of God says.

They are not missing it in believing the Word.

They *are missing* it by not knowing how to walk in love.

You see, faith is the hand that takes the things we need from God. Everything Jesus purchased for us on Calvary can be obtained by faith. But faith works by *love.*

Jesus purchased for us salvation, healing, the fullness of the Spirit, the gifts of the Spirit, the fruit of the recreated spirit, and victory over the world, the flesh, the devil, and all the powers of darkness. All of these things come to us by faith — but it must be faith that works by love (Gal. 5:6).

Faith teaching has been strong for many years now. We have been hearing faith, healing, prosperity, and all of these great truths preached from the Word of God.

I realize that teachers sometime overstate certain things to make a point, but we are in danger of becoming overbalanced in the area of faith. We are not getting some of the other basic teachings that should go along with having faith.

Many people have the mistaken idea that just because they are walking the faith walk, they are never going to have any trials. But they didn't get that idea from my father, Rev. Kenneth E. Hagin, who many consider the modern-day father of faith.

If you study his material carefully, you will discover that concept never came from him. Some people who are teaching his materials are saying things he never said — things they cannot back up with the Word of God.

One of the reasons why faith is not working for some is that they do not have a full understanding of what the Word of God says. Faith that works by love will measure up to all of the standards set down in the Word of God.

Anyone can take several Old Testament scriptures, add some New Testament scriptures, and "prove" that it is right to do just about anything. But that doesn't make it right! You can create any doctrine you want by pulling scriptures out of context. But you couldn't prove your doctrine if you included the preceding and proceeding verses in the context.

Part of the love walk is being able to stand up and preach what God's Word says, not some doctrine created from isolated scriptures.

For a while, because of some kind of wrong teaching, people got so much into "positive confessions" that they couldn't even make a statement in fun. Certainly, we need to be careful about our confessions, but we need to be even more careful about our daily lives.

You see, we become accustomed to doing certain things in the natural that we never realize could be hindering us in the spiritual — things like losing our temper! To make faith work in our lives, we must protect ourselves in every area.

Bible teachers say we must have faith to please God, but many casually pass over the teachings that *faith works by love.*

When I was a boy, there were more various subjects preached than what I hear now. One was the power in the blood of Jesus. Another was this subject of love. All of these doctrines must fit together.

If we are to live in line with God's Word, we must not only be a faith child of a faith God, but we must be a *love* child of a *love* God!

Many Bible teachers have left it for people to pick up this teaching themselves, but many believers have not. Too many Christians lose knowledge about walking in love. We need to understand all facets of the love walk and how it relates to success in life, both spiritually and naturally. The love of God needs to ooze out of us so much that when we enter a room, people will know we are walking in love!

If we are going to make this faith house strong, we must make its foundation strong. It is time we began to teach the *full* Gospel, not just part of the Gospel. It is time we began to teach how to live a life of love.

Balancing the Message

Most people do not like to hear about the love message, and most preachers do not like to preach it, because it is not "exciting." It searches deep into the hearts of the listeners. Exciting messages and times of rejoicing are wonderful, but if we are to mature, we must stay balanced according to the Word.

The Kingdom of God has been damaged by people who have heard the faith message once and then have run off without really knowing what they had heard. Before long, they came crashing down and didn't understand why. Someone could show them from the Word where they went wrong — if they would listen.

Similarly, when some people start studying the love message, they try to digest too much at once. They run off on a tangent with it and get it all out of proportion. For example, they think that walking in love means being a "doormat." We have to try to explain it. This is the enemy's way to thwart us from receiving God's best for our life and fulfilling our divine destiny. However, if taken in the proper dosage and tempered with the Spirit of God, a study of God's love can show you the best way to live.

(I realize I am presenting the other side of the faith message, but it is time that someone did. It doesn't do you any good for me to talk about taking back what the devil's stolen and building strong faith unless I also talk about love — because *faith works by love*! This study will show some of you why things are perhaps not happening in your life — things you have been confessing and believing for.)

I'm going to make a statement here that I want you to think about: You can be in the family of God, and still not walk in the perfect law of love. (It's like being in the family of God and not walking in faith.)

Many Christians will go to Heaven, but they won't have any reward. Paul was referring to people who never grow in various areas of their Christian walk and never attain to a high degree of spirituality. All of our works will be tried by fire (1 Cor. 3:13).

Read about the Corinthians. Never was there a more carnal group of Christians! That is why we get so much of our teaching out of the epistles to the Corinthians; Paul had to deal with so much carnality among them.

I'm sure if we began to be honest with ourselves and began to measure ourselves with God's love, every one of us would have to mark a big "F" (for failure) on the top of our personal score sheet.

Do you know why? Not because we are failing willfully, but because the Gospel has not been fully preached as it should have been.

We can't do anything about the past. That's history. But we can change the future. As for me and my house, we are going to secure all the promises of God, because *faith worketh by love!*

The kind of love I'm talking about will take the Word of God in your heart and in your mouth and turn it into a steamroller for God! Nothing will be able to stand in your way — nothing whatsoever. You will roll right over obstacles. If the devil stands in your way, you will turn on the love of God and roll right over him, praising Jesus all the while! You will begin to see things happen.

The Bible says demons believe and even tremble (James 2:19) — but they never receive anything. Why? Because they don't have any love. They are filled with hate and fear.

What Does Love Do?

Because we must have faith that works by love, it would be well for us to see how that kind of love gets started and what its characteristics are.

Proverbs 10:12 says, *". . . love covereth all sins."* First Peter 4:8 says, *". . . charity* [or love] *shall cover a multitude of sins."* Put these two scriptures together, and they say, "Love covers all sins, even when there is a multitude of them."

Love must begin to work with the sin problem. Love will not work for you until you are born again and the love of God has removed your sins.

Notice the phrase "a multitude of sins." How many is a multitude? Don't we usually use the word "multitude" when there are more elements to something than we can name?

Think of it: This real, genuine love of God will cover, hide, and put out of sight more sins than we can even name. What a tremendous thought!

"For God so loved the world, that he gave his only begotten Son . . ." (John 3:16). Why did God give His Son? To remit and forgive our sins. That's the first area of love — God's love covers and removes sin.

Many people are saying to sinners, "You need to confess every sin you've ever committed." They talk about "inner healing." They say, "You need to go back and drag out all the sins from your past and confess them."

No, you don't! You couldn't remember every sin you ever committed. All you need to do is get the love of God to hide or remove that multitude of sins in the New Birth. Dragging up your old sins will not do you any good; it will just bring condemnation — and you've got enough of that already with the sins you *can* remember.

Living First Corinthians 13

Now let us look at some "real life" examples of ways to put First Corinthians 13 to work in our life.

GALATIANS 6:1
1 Brethren, if a man be overtaken in a fault, ye which are spiritual, restore such an one in the spirit of meekness; considering thyself, lest thou also be tempted.

Notice the phrase, "restore such a one in the spirit of *meekness*." Meekness is one of the fruits of the recreated human spirit (Gal. 5:23). Then look at another phrase, "lest thou also be tempted." In other words, unless you show love in some of these areas, you might be taken in by the same things.

The first thing most people want to do when they hear of someone being overtaken in a fault is reach for the telephone! They don't want to cover that fault with love and silence or restore the individual; they want to talk about him and his fault.

Then in the next breath, they say, "Oh, Lord, I want to confess that I have the money I need." Well, that confession is not going to work! They don't have love working in their life — and faith works by love. *If we do not operate in the fullness of love, then our faith will not operate in its fullest capacity.*

As we saw in First Peter, love covers a multitude of sins, including all those we can't even name. Think of it. Love covers sin — and sin is the worst thing in the universe! Sin separates us from God. God's love covers that sin.

We learn something about God's love from "The Love Chapter," First Corinthians 13. (This chapter is actually part of a discourse of First Corinthians 12, 13, and 14 combined.)

When you consider chapter 13 in context, you will see that even the gifts of the Spirit must be operated with love or they become empty.

In chapter 13, "love" is translated "charity." Verse 7 says "love beareth all things." Another translation reads, "love covers all things with silence." Thus,

God is saying that love not only *hides* the sin and evil of others; it *refuses to speak of it.*

If we tell of the evil someone has done, or if we criticize, judge, condemn, or murmur against him — no matter who he is or what he has done — we are proving we are not walking in love. Why? Because love covers with silence.

Jesus showed perfect love when He forgave those who were responsible for sending Him to the Cross. He prayed, ". . . *Father, forgive them; for they know not what they do* . . ." (Luke 23:34). Jesus was love personified.

Some people think God has given them "the gift of exposing." Human nature is that way. Even though we know God has forgiven a person, some people can never forgive him.

Watch What You Say

I knew a man not long ago who was doing a tremendous job for God when someone came into his congregation and said, "Do you know what your pastor did before he was saved?" He exposed the pastor's past.

The man accusing the pastor was supposed to be a good Christian. (When someone does this, I question his standing with God according to the Word.)

How often a stupid remark from some so-called Christian has caused problems for people. Without realizing it, the accuser is bringing destruction on his own head, because he is not walking in love.

We must not allow ourselves to talk about people. We must cover sin with a love that silences our mouths. While this God-kind of love covers the sins of others with silence, it does not cover our sins and wrongdoings with silence. We must confess them to the Father.

God says in Proverbs 28:13 that we will not prosper if we cover our sins: *"He that covereth his sins shall not prosper: but whoso confesseth and forsaketh them shall have mercy."*

Frequently, we put God's plan in reverse. We want to use love to cover up our own wrongdoings, but we want to expose someone else's. We rationalize by saying, "Oh, I'm not condemning him; I'm merely making an observation." Then we say, "I'm confessing that the Lord is going to meet all my needs." Well, we might as well forget about that confession and find some way to meet that need ourselves, because we just cut the lifeline between God and us. We violated the law of love.

First Corinthians 13 also tells us that love *". . . suffereth long, and is kind . . . envieth not . . ."* (v. 4). From this scripture we are told that love works by being kind even under *long-suffering* brought on by someone else. I don't mean sickness, suffering, or disease brought on by the devil; I mean suffering caused by other people, such as remarks made about you.

Horrible remarks are made about people when they choose to serve Christ and follow in the fullness of the Word of God. Some people are even excommunicated from their churches and families.

Many RHEMA students suffer long because someone they know is continually telling them how stupid they are to leave their homes and go away to a Bible school. After awhile, this can start to hurt.

This is where love really has to work, because you must love those people, keep your mouth shut, endure, and be kind.

Perhaps you will encounter the very person who was responsible for getting you kicked out of your church. Walk up to that person, smile, and say, "Hello. How are you? We love everyone in the church and just want to tell you how much we love and appreciate you."

Of course, you would *like* to say, "Why don't you keep your mouth shut? You don't know what you're talking about." But that is not the way of love.

You must pray, "Lord, bless them. Lord, help them. They don't know what they are doing. Help them because they do not understand."

I had to learn this myself when people said nasty things about my father's ministry — the ministry I am tied to by my very birth. They even have called it a "faith cult."

Now, it is difficult enough for me to say, "Lord, forgive them" when people take verbal shots at *me*, but when they start accusing my *family*, that's another story. It is very difficult to "suffer long" when things are said against my father. I know he has done what God asked him to do through the years, and he did without many material comforts early in his ministry because he would not compromise.

I have learned that if I am to maintain any kind of faith walk, I must put down my carnal nature. The secret is letting the love of God work within my spirit.

Yes, slanderous remarks are hurtful, and if you are not careful, you will cut off people who said them about you. If you see them at a convention, you will manage to be busy talking to someone else. When they start walking in your direction, you conveniently have to stop in the bookstore, or you conveniently see someone you think you know across the auditorium — and you take off between the rows of chairs to get out of the aisle they're coming down. Love does not do that.

One of the hardest things I ever had to do was stand in an exhibition hall and talk to a young minister who had made hurtful remarks about me.

When I was getting started in the ministry, this young minister would hardly speak to me. Now as my own ministry grew and developed, he was inviting me to come and preach in his big church.

It would have been so easy to have told him off, but the next week my pocketbook would have suffered. I live by faith personally. I am also responsible for believing for the operating expenses of RHEMA Bible Training Center (I have many others believing with me too). I know that if I start walking out of love, my faith will be hindered. It will not operate to its fullest capacity.

I can make all the confessions I want to. I can quote the Bible day and night. I can fast and pray — and I still won't get anything if I'm walking out of love!

The Word of God says faith *worketh by love*. If we're not walking in love, our faith won't work!

The Fruit of the Spirit

As we study the fruit of the spirit, we find that we cannot have any of the fruit operating in our life until we have love. I think this is the reason love is listed first in Galatians 5:22. It is the foundation on which the rest of the fruit of the spirit rests.

When "faith people" wake up and start checking all areas of their lives, they will find certain areas in which they are not really walking in love — and these areas are hindering their faith from operating to its fullest capacity.

Love envieth not. Love does not desire position, honor, power, benefits, favor, esteem, or blessings that others have. Love is more interested in what it can do to help others get more than what it has itself.

When you begin to operate in this realm of love, you cannot help but receive for yourself. When you are involved in helping someone else, you automatically will be promoted, because promotion comes from God. It is just like when you come into God's law of prosperity. As you give, it will be given unto you.

The kind of love I'm talking about does not get upset when other people get good things — it gets excited. It rejoices. (I realize that when you start teaching like this, the world thinks you are crazy, but that is the kind of love we must have if our faith is to work.)

Love is not puffed up. Love does not think more highly of itself than it should. It doesn't think, *Why did the pastor put him in that position? I've been around longer than he has. I've got more gifts of the Spirit in operation than he does. I don't understand it. I've got better ideas than he does.*

No, love does not think "I know more." Love says, "I'll get behind this person and work with him. Even if I know more than he does, I'll feed him ideas and make him look good, because I know things that will help this group grow." (The problem with human nature is that people don't want to share their ideas because they want to get all the credit for themselves.)

The charismatic movement today has more problems in this area of love than in any other. I'm talking about pure love — the love of God — not someone's thought-up doctrine. I'm talking about the kind of love outlined in Philippians 2:3,4: *"Let nothing be done through strife or vainglory; but in lowliness of mind let each esteem other better than themselves. Look not every man on his own things, but every man also on the things of others."*

We must not esteem ourselves better than another, and we must not think more highly of ourselves than we ought. This can bring us down in a hurry. Many people have been brought low because of this.

Some people have lost everything they had. People have said, "The Lord had to take it all away from them so He could work out something in their life." No, that is not what happened. The reason they lost it is because they didn't know how to love, and this opened the door for the devil. He came in and wrought havoc in their life. God didn't have a thing to do with it. He could not keep the devil from destroying them, because they were not walking in love.

Love seeketh not her own. Romans 12:10 tells us, *"Be kindly affectioned one to another with brotherly love; in honour preferring one another."* When we get so busy preferring everyone else and unselfishly helping them obtain blessings that we forget about ourselves, that's when we will find honor, success, and promotion for ourself.

Many ministers would like to preach in one of our large seminars or Campmeetings. It is worthwhile to check the histories of those who do. You will find they have been interested in helping others succeed — sometimes at the expense of their own ministry.

Other people have gotten started in ministry because of my dad's ministry. They'll even admit it. They have preached his sermons almost verbatim from his tapes.

Dad just says, "Bless God, more power to them. If they can preach it better than I can, that's great." *In honor preferring one another.*

Someone once asked me what the secret of my father's success was. I replied, "One of the secrets of Kenneth E. Hagin's success is that he walks in perfect love.

"He is not afraid to prefer his brother before himself. He is not afraid of another person's ministry. And I'm not talking about a little ministry that is just getting started; I'm talking about well-known ministries.

"He is not afraid to sit down, take the back seat, and let another minister take his own service.

"This is the faith that works by love!"

I have been in services where the Spirit of God started to move on someone to use him, and the scheduled speaker got nervous. He didn't want anyone to disturb "his" service. He said, "This is my meeting, bless God, and no one is going to get up on that platform but me!"

This quenched the Spirit. The speaker's message went over like the proverbial lead balloon. *Love seeketh not her own.*

It's easy to do this with God too. "Now, Father, you know all the things I've been doing for You. I drove a hundred miles this week just teaching prayer groups. You know I've been giving so much time and money." Without realizing it, you are saying, "It's time You did something for me." But love does not seek her own. Love is interested in helping.

Love Doesn't Get Offended

Love is not easily provoked. That means love does not get angry easily. Psalm 119:165 says, *"Great peace have they which love thy law: and nothing shall offend them."* The words "offend" and "provoke" are interchangeable.

Love is not easily provoked even when people say, "The reason Hagin is going to work for his daddy is because he hasn't got any other place to go." Love is not easily provoked!

Love responds, "Lord, help them. They don't understand what they're doing. Forgive them, because they are putting themselves in jeopardy."

When I was active in high school sports, our coaches quickly found out just what to say to motivate each fellow on the team.

They knew they could easily provoke me by telling me I was a decent player, but that I couldn't surpass my opponents. They would say, "Now, Hagin, you are going to have to do the best you can. Try to hold your own. There is no way you can overtake them."

When I was running, the track coach used to do that all the time, and when I was playing wide receiver, the football coach used to tell me I could not beat some of the defensive backs. I would be so provoked that when I got to the game, I guarantee you, I was going to show them all!

My coaches knew how to manage me in the natural, and there's nothing wrong with that. But the devil also knows how to get us provoked, and when he provokes us, his intentions are to get us off-track spiritually. We might say, "Bless God, I'm going out there and I'm going to do such-and-such," and we think we're being spiritual. But that is not the spirit of meekness or gentleness. You can't have meekness or gentleness if you don't have love.

Love Speaks No Evil

Love thinketh no evil. Love covers sin with silence and will not speak of it. It refuses to think about it. Sometimes you can't help what you overhear — but you can refuse to repeat it or think about it. Cast it out of your mind. Love thinks on the truth, the good, the lovely.

My father-in-law tells a story about a man who never said anything bad about anyone in his whole life. He just wouldn't.

Then the worst man in the community died. There wasn't anything good about him at all. He was mean, and he had lived the worst life of just about anyone.

Several people from the community were standing around the casket waiting for this particular man to come by. What would he say about the deceased?

Finally he came. He stood and stood and looked and looked.

The others couldn't stand it any longer. "Well, what do you think?" they asked anxiously.

He gazed into the casket. Finally, he looked up and said, "Well, he did have pretty teeth, didn't he?"

He had found something good to say! If you have to stand there until you can find something good to say about someone, do it. Even if it's nothing more than, "They have a nice part in their hair," or "Their glasses are very becoming." Say something good.

Paul talks about this in Philippians.

PHILIPPIANS 4:8
8 Finally, brethren, whatsoever things are true, whatsoever things are honest, whatsoever things are just, whatsoever things are pure, whatsoever things are lovely, whatsoever things are of good report; if there be any virtue, and if there be any praise, think on these things.

Do not entertain bad thoughts about anyone. It will hinder your love walk and your faith — and that will keep you from receiving what you need from God and from fulfilling your divine destiny!

Love endureth all things. What does "endure" mean in this case? It means to go through all kinds of trying, hurtful, evil, slanderous experiences — calmly, sweetly, silently, lovingly, uncomplainingly — as if they weren't happening.

"Endureth all things" means putting up with just about anything. Did you ever realize how much a pastor has to endure? He has to put up with all of the people who sit in the congregation — along with all of their little idiosyncrasies!

Some of the worst things that have ever happened to a believer have not been to be shot with a gun, hit with a fist, or cut with a knife. They have been the result of the tongues of other Christians!

The same individuals who take their tongue and cut someone to ribbons will come to church the next night, get up, and testify about how much they love God. Then they will quote the Word of God and say, "My God shall supply all my needs. By His stripes I am healed."

They will make all the right confessions and wonder why no money comes in and why sickness stays with them.

It's very simple. They are not walking in love. And when you are not walking in love, the law of faith is not going to work for you.

Do you want perfect faith? Learn to walk in love. When you begin to walk the love walk, your faith will be perfected.

Do you want guaranteed answers to your prayers? Learn to live a life of love.

God is love. He has imparted His love to us. If we learn how to operate in the law of love, the law of faith will work in us, because *faith worketh by love*. (The law of faith will not work in us *until* we operate in the law of love.)

My faith works because I have love. I do not have love because I have faith — it's the other way around. I have *faith* because I have *love*. This is the kind of faith that God has. This is the kind of faith that will prevail.

Yes, making confessions of faith is good — we've got to do that — but if you stop and find an area where you can love more, you will begin to see your faith work more.

Find a place to start showing love. That means more than just giving someone a hug. It may mean helping some bum in the gutter. That's the way love is. Instead of trying to *get* love all the time, love *gives*.

I look around to see how I can help someone obtain something they may need. Faith works by love, and as I make my love work, my faith will bring me more and more.

Sometimes we get so excited about faith that we act in presumption instead of real faith. Faith that is not founded on a good foundation always will act in presumption. Faith founded on the Word of God always will act in line with God's Word and will not do anything foolish.

Dream 'Faith' Dreams!

The God-kind of faith is tempered by love.

You can't do anything without love. The gifts of the Spirit will not operate properly if you don't have love. You will not have faith enough to combat Satan if you don't have love.

But when you get this kind of love, you will not be content to be mediocre, stay in a corner, and barely make it to Heaven. You will be a success even when you are not trying to be!

Think of all the marvelous, blessed things God has prepared for us! We could sit and dream and dream and dream of them.

Dream faith dreams! When you put the love of God to work with your faith and your confession, you will watch those dreams turn into realities!

Can you afford *not* to live a life of love? Can you afford to hold one bit of malice? Can you afford not to love your neighbor as yourself? Can you afford not to love yourself?

Did you know that you cannot love other people until you love yourself. God said you must love your neighbor *as yourself.* People protest, "Oh, I don't want to be arrogant. We're supposed to be humble!" There is a difference between being arrogant and loving yourself — a great deal of difference. You can be arrogant and still not love yourself. And you can be humble and at the same time love yourself according to the Word of God.

You should know who you are in Christ, what you are in Christ, and what you have in Christ. Knowing that believers are kings who sit in heavenly places with Christ will give you a good self-image!

Do you know what is wrong with many marriages? Two people who can't even love themselves are trying to love one another. How can they love their mate if they can't love themselves?

Love in Action

Jesus showed ultimate love when He took a piece of bread at the Last Supper, dipped it into the common dish, and fed it to Judas with His very fingers — knowing all the while that this man was betraying him (John 13:26)! That is love. According to the custom of their day, the highest act of love one could perform was to feed bread to a friend with his own fingers.

Another demonstration of Jesus' love is seen in Matthew 23:37 when He wept over Jerusalem, the city that had persecuted Him more than any other — the city He loved more than any other.

Notice also how Jesus honored Peter, who had lost his nerve and denied ever knowing Jesus. Jesus distinguished Peter from the other disciples in the message the angel delivered: "*. . . go your way, tell his disciples AND PETER. . .*" (Mark 16:7). That is love.

We as Christians are called to love the unlovely. Most of us, however, want the unlovely to straighten up first. *Then* we are willing to help them. But it isn't going to work that way.

This God-kind of love will spill over into your job, your school, and every other aspect of your life. Not only will you reap spiritual benefits; you will reap natural benefits you've never thought possible. Your fellow employees will think you are one of the most wonderful people in the world, and they will see to it that you get the benefits and promotions you deserve.

Yes, when you get your life and your actions lined up with the Word of God, and you place a strong guard on your tongue, you soon will find the love walk becoming automatic.

When someone provokes you and you feel the old nature start to rise up inside of you, you will find yourself saying, "Praise the Lord. I love you." You will find yourself growing spiritually.

You will wake up one morning and find that good things are happening to you. Promotions are coming. The money you need is coming. Everything you need is coming to you.

Then it will dawn on you that while you are living a life of love, you are not having to make all these good things happen — they are happening automatically as you walk in love.

Your faith is strong, and faith worketh by love — God's love — and that love covers the sins, mistakes, and shortcomings of others.

This is the way to fulfill your divine destiny and accomplish God's plan for your life.

We need to realize that as Christians, we all have a common destiny, and that God's plan for our lives is salvation, healing, deliverance, prosperity, and everything that pertains to life and godliness.

Once you realize these things, then you can start accomplishing God's plan for your life by attending to God's Word, being led by the Spirit of God, learning to forgive, taking back what the devil's stolen, building strong faith, and living a life of love.

If you listen to many of those around you, they'll keep you in bondage. If you read the Word of God through the rose-tinted glasses of tradition, you'll remain in bondage. But if you open your eyes wide to the truth of God's Word, you can change your destiny! If your destiny is changed, it will be because you realize the truth of God's Word, and you get up and walk in it.

Find out what God wants from you, and do it. I challenge you: Receive what God has for you! It belongs to you. Don't let the devil or any person take it away from you. Your divine destiny awaits you!

About the Author

Rev. Kenneth W. Hagin, President of Kenneth Hagin Ministries and pastor of RHEMA Bible Church, ministers around the world. Known for calling the Body of Christ to steadfast faith, he seizes every ministry opportunity to impart an attitude of "I cannot be defeated, and I will not quit."

Rev. Hagin began preparing for his call to ministry— a ministry that now spans almost 50 years—at Southwestern Assemblies of God University. He graduated from Oral Roberts University in Tulsa, Oklahoma, and holds an honorary Doctor of Divinity degree from Faith Theological Seminary in Tampa, Florida.

In his early years of ministry, Rev. Hagin was an associate pastor and traveling evangelist. Later, he went on to organize and develop RHEMA Bible Training Centers in Broken Arrow, Oklahoma, and in 13 countries around the world.

Rev. Hagin's array of responsibilities also includes International Director of RHEMA Ministerial Association International. With his wife, Rev. Lynette Hagin, he co-hosts *Rhema for Today*, a weekday radio program broadcast throughout the United States, and *RHEMA Praise*, a weekly television broadcast.

Recognizing the lateness of the hour before the second coming of the Lord Jesus Christ, Rev. Hagin has expanded his speaking schedule beyond his regular pastoral duties. To fulfill the urgent call of God to prepare the Church for a deeper experience of His Presence, Rev. Hagin delivers messages that reveal key spiritual truths about faith, healing, and other vital subjects. He often ministers with a strong healing anointing, and his ministry helps lead believers into a greater experience of the Glory of God!

Rev. Hagin and his wife live in Tulsa, Oklahoma. He is the son of the late Kenneth E. Hagin.

God has a *specific* plan for your life.
Are you ready?
RHEMA Bible Training Center

> ". . . Giving all *diligence*, add to your faith *virtue*,
> to virtue *knowledge* . . . .
> For if these things are yours and *abound*,
> you will be neither barren nor *unfruitful*
> in the knowledge of our Lord Jesus Christ."
> —2 Peter 1:5,8 (*NKJV*)

- Take your place in the Body of Christ for the last great revival.
- Learn to rightly divide God s Word and hear His voice clearly.
- Discover how to be a willing vessel for God s glory.
- Receive practical hands-on ministry training from experienced ministers.

*Qualified instructors are waiting to teach, train, and help **you** to fulfill your destiny!*

Call today for information or application material.
1-888-28-FAITH (1-888-283-2484)
Offer #BKORD:PRMDRBTC

www.rbtc.org

Call now to receive a *free* subscription to *The Word of Faith* magazine from Kenneth Hagin Ministries. Receive encouragement and spiritual refreshment from . . .

- *Faith-building articles from Rev. Kenneth W. Hagin, Rev. Lynette Hagin, and others*
- *Timeless Teaching from the archives of Rev. Kenneth E. Hagin*
- *Monthly features on prayer and healing*
- *Testimonies of salvation, healing, and deliverance*
- *Children s activity page*
- *Updates on RHEMA Bible Training Center, RHEMA Bible Church, and other outreaches of Kenneth Hagin Ministries*

FREE

Subscribe today!

1-888-28-FAITH (1-888-283-2484)

www.rhema.org/wof

Offer #BKORD:WF